SAMURAI TRAILS

SAMURAI TRAILS

Wanderings on the Japanese High Road

LUCIAN SWIFT KIRTLAND

EDITED BY WILLIAM DE LANGE

TOYO REFERENCE SERIES

First edition, 2017

Published by TOYO Press

Copyright © 2017 TOYO Press

ISBN 978-94-92722-010

Table of Contents

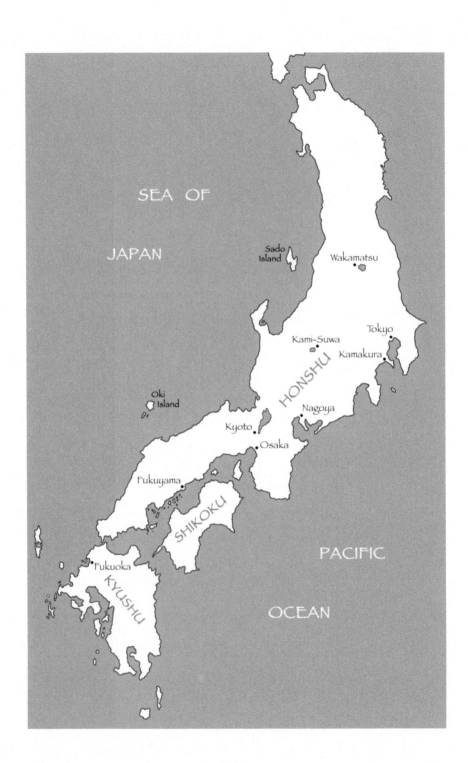

SEA OF

JAPAN

Sado
Island

Wakamatsu

Tokyo

Kami-Suwa

Kamakura

HONSHU

Oki
Island

Nagoya

Kyoto

Osaka

Fukuyama

SHIKOKU

PACIFIC

Fukuoka

OCEAN

KYUSHU

Foreword

It was spring and it was Spain. Sunset brought the white-haired custodian of the Court of the Lions to the balcony overhanging my fountain. His blue coat bespoke officialdom but his Andalusian lisp veiled this suggestion of compulsion. His wishes for my evening's happiness, nevertheless, were to be interpreted as a request for my going. The Alhambra had to be locked up for the night.

I was lying outstretched on the stones of Lindaroxa's Court with my head against a pillar. The last light of the April sun had scaled the walls and was losing itself among the top-most bobbing oranges of Lindaroxa's tree. To dream there must be to have one's dreams come true, some inheritance from Moorish alchemy.

Despite the setting, I was not dreaming of the Alhambra, not even of Lindaroxa. I was thinking of a friend of irresponsible imagination but of otherwise responsibility. I was wondering where he could be. On the previous summer we had walked the highroads of England and I had found him a most satisfying disputatious companion of enquiring mind. We had talked somewhat of a similar wandering in Japan, a vagabondage free from cicerones and away from the touristic places, but although we had treated this plan with due respect, we had never an idea of transmuting it into action.

The Alhambra had to be locked up for the night. The custodian bowed low, and I bowed low, in unhurried obligation to dignity, and I walked away to my inn. There I found a cablegram from America. It read:

"Can meet you Kyoto June two months' walking."

It was signed by the other dreamer of the Two-Sworded Trails.

I cabled back, "yes." The message gone, I awoke to the reality of time and space. All Europe, Siberia, Manchuria, and Korea spread out their distances on the map and were lying between me and the keeping of my promise.

It was in the darkness of midnight and it was raining when I stepped off the express to the Kyoto platform. For a month the world had been revolving giddily under railway carriage succeeding railway carriage until it seemed that the changing peoples outside the car windows could be taking on their ceaseless variety only through some illusion within my own eyes.

I stood for a while in the shelter of the overhanging, dripping roof of the Kyoto station awaiting some providential development, but probably the local god of wayfarers did not judge my plight worry of special interposition. Finally I found a drenched youth in a stupor of sleep between the shafts of his *rikisha*. His dreams were evidently depressing, for he awoke with appreciation for the escape. We bent over his paper lantern and at last coaxed a spurt of flame from a box of unspeakable matches. (The government decrees that matches must be given away and not sold by the tobacconists. Japan's spirit of the art of giving should not be judged by this item. The generosity is in the acceptance of the matches.) I climbed into the *rikisha* and stowed myself away under the hood, naming the inn which had been appointed by cablegram for the meeting place. The boy pattered along in his straw sandals at full speed through the mist, shouting hoarsely at the corners. At last he dug his heels into the pebbles and stopped, and pounded at the inn door until someone came and slid back the bolts.

Yes, a guest with the name of Owre had arrived that day at noon and had sat up for me until midnight. He had left word that I should be taken to his room. Thus I was led through dark halls until we came to the door. We pushed it open and called into the darkness. Back came a welcome—somewhat sleepy. The clerk struck a match and I discovered my vagabond companion crawling out from under the mosquito netting of his four-poster. Between us we had covered twenty thousand miles for that handshake.

"It's the moment to be highly dramatic," he said with an eloquent flourish of his pajam'd arm, and he sent the clerk for a bottle of native beer. It came, warm and of infinite foam, but we managed to find a few drops of liquid at the bottom with which to drink a toast. The toast was to "The Road."

The Quest for Hori-san

After our melodramatic toast of the night before it would have been only orthodox to have said goodbye to our Occidental inn at sunrise and to have sought the road. But we had a call to make. The fulfilling of the obligation proved to be momentous. There is one never-to-be-broken rule for the foreigner in the Orient: He must consider himself always to be of extreme magnitude in the perspective, and any action which concerns himself is momentous. If Asia had possessed this supreme self-concern, she might today be playing political chess with colonies in Europe. The details of our call are thus set down in faithful sequence.

"If ever you come to Japan, be sure to look me up." This had been the farewell of Hori Kenjirō when he said goodbye to his university days in America. Kenjirō's affection for America had had the vigor which marks the vitality of Japanese loyalty. He had always singled out our better qualities with gratifying disregard for opposites.

We were, however, without an address except that we thought he might be in Kobe. But it seemed unreasonable that after travelling all the way to the Antipodes we should then be baulked by a mere detail. In the faith of this logic we took an early train to Kobe, and the first sign that we saw read: "Information Bureau for Foreigners."

The man in uniform peering out of the box window was so smiling and so evidently desirous of being helpful that whether we had needed information or not, it would have been exceedingly discourteous not to have asked some question. We inquired the address of Dr. Hori Kenjirō. The information dispenser thumbed all his heap of directories. He appeared

1

to be unravelling his thread by a most intricate system of cross reference. Then he looked at us with another smile.

"Did you find it?" we asked.

"I find no address," he said, "but I tell *rikisha* boys take you. Ah, so!"

Such a challenge was impossible to refuse. We got into the *rikisha* and the men bent their necks and jerked the wheels into motion with strange disregard for any bee-line direction to any particular place. It appeared to be a most casual choice whether we took one corner or another. This rambling went on for some time. Suddenly they held back on the shafts and said: "Here!" We were at the door of a wholesale importing house. No one within had ever heard of *o*-Hori-*san*. When we came back to the street with this information the coolies seemed not at all surprised. They shrugged their shoulders at our mild expostulation as if implying, "Of course, if he isn't here he must be some other place."

After another panting dash they stopped and said: "Here!" It was obvious without inquiring that Kenjirō could not be in that shallow, open-fronted shop. "Very well," the shoulders answered us and on we went. We stopped for another time with the now familiar "Here!" We had traversed half Kobe. Our futile questions seemed to have nothing to do with any next step. Strangely, instead of having lost our faith it had been growing that by some system the coolies were following the quest. At this stop, when we looked inside the entrance, there was the name of Dr. Hori Kenjirō on a brass plate. We walked up the stairs and rang a bell and inquired for Dr. Hori of the boy who came.

We asked him to tell *o*-Hori-*san* that *o*-Owre-*san* and *o*-Kirt-land-*san* would like to see him. Of all arrangements of consonants (w's, r's, k's, and l's) to harass the Japanese tongue, our two names stand in the first group of the first list of impossibles. We could overhear the distressed boy's struggle with "*o*-Owre-*san*." I was impressed that from that instant Owre Alfred became "*o*-Owre-*san*." It was a secular confirmation too positive to be gainsaid.[1]

---

[1] The adding of the honorific suffix "*san*" to one's name when introducing oneself is a typical mistake made by those first visiting Japan, but extremely jarring to the Japanese ear, finely attuned as it is to their use. For readability all occurrences are hereafter dropped, as well as the honorific prefix "*o*," and both of Kirtland's travel companions are referred to by their first names.

Small wonder then that Kenjirō had not the slightest idea who was waiting at the door. But his surprise, when he appeared, was so smoothed out and repressed in his formal *samurai* welcome that we were tempted into moody thinking that through some psychosis the frightful slaughter of our names had destroyed his remembrance of our rightful personalities.

Friends appeared and were introduced with ceremonial formalism. We sat in a circle and sipped iced mineral water. Kenjirō inquired politely of our plans and then sat back in silence behind his thick spectacles. The icy temperature of the mineral water was the temperature of the verve of the conversation. The day itself was rather hot; a damp, depressing heat. I tried to fan off the flies which stuck tenaciously with sharp, sudden buzzings.

Of all varieties of uncreative activity, the analyzing of moods brings the least compensation—but that does not mean avoidance. During that hour a disturbing remoteness to everyday reality rasped as if something untoward had been conjured up. Alfred and I talked, trying to explain our plans. We repeated that we hadn't any desire to visit the great places, but our saying so sounded childish and impertinent,—very tiresome. A dignified ancient kept forcing us into a position of defense. To put us out of ease was his most remote wish, of course, but he did insist with patriotic eloquence (suggesting a Californian defending his climate) that the show places deserved to be paid respect. We insisted that our tourist consciences had been appeased long before, and that we now intended to run away from foreign hotels, from the Honorable Society of Guides, from the Imperial Welcome Society, from all cicerones, and from all centers where the customs and conveniences of our Western variety of civilization are so cherishingly catered to.

"But," interrupted Kenjirō, "you do not understand. You will find no one prepared for foreigners. You will find not one word of English. You must not do such a thing." With Japan so earnestly providing the proper accommodations at the proper places, it was not playing the game, so to speak, to refuse.

When an argument of policy is between an amateur and an expert (particularly so when between a foreigner and a native) the tyro can afford to compromise on not one atom of his ignorance. If he concedes at all he will be overwhelmed completely. We refused Kenjirō's warnings, remaining impervious to any advice which did not further our plan of action exactly as outlined.

"Very well, then," said Kenjirō, "I shall have to go with you."

Under the excitement of talking plans Kenjirō slipped out of his formalism, and became exactly his old-time self. Until the following week, however, he would not be able to turn his solicitude into action. He did not lose his cataclysm of positive doubt over entrusting the Empire in our hands, but as there was no escape from leaving us to our own devices for those days (and we made known a certain vanity in our own resources) he at length agreed to meet us in Nagoya, and we planned a route which would bring us there with our rendezvous at the European hotel.

The Ancient Tōkaidō

It was the morning of our last sleep in *seiyō-jin* beds. I dreamed that I was still dreaming in Lindaroxa's Court. Alfred shook my four-poster and begged me to consider the matter-of-factness of rolling out from my mosquito netting and taking a bite of cold breakfast. The sensuous breeze of the East, which comes for a brief hour with the first light of the sun, was blowing the curtains back from the window. I was willing to consider the getting up and the eating of the breakfast and I was willing to call both endeavours matter-of-fact, but the imagination that it was to be the first day on the highroad belonged to no such mere negativity of living.

I began packing and was inspired to improvise a wonderful ballad. It was concerned with the beginning of trails. Alfred was busy and was uninterested in my stanzas. He might very well have served genius by taking them down. The all-inclusiveness embraced, I remember, a master picture of cold dawn in the Rockies, with pack ponies snorting, biting, and bucking. And I sang blithely of every other sort of first morning start, embroidering the memories of their roaring language and their unpackable dunnage. But in Japan one does not roar—or one roars alone—and I had known just what was going into my rucksack for weeks.

Our route was to be the famed Tōkaidō, that ancient road running between the great capitals of the West and the East, from Kyoto to Tokyo. We were to find its first stretch at the turn to the left when we should cross the bridge over the Kamo River. This river cuts Kyoto between two long rows of houses built on piles and overhanging its waters. In summer the stream is most domesticated and gives, charitably, a large area of its dry bed as a pleasure ground for *fêtes*, but when the snows are melting back in the hills in the days of spring and blossoms, it becomes temperamental and the peasants say that it has drunk unwisely of *sake*. It is then that the water winks rakishly and splashes the tips of its waves at pretty *geisha*, who come to scatter cherry petals on the current. But we saw only the summer domesticity on our June morning. A school of children were wading in the shallow current, fishing with nets. Their *yukata* were tied high above their sturdy fat legs. We leaned over the rail and they squinted back into the sun at us and called out good-morning. Then we stepped off the bridge and our boots were on the long road that leads to Tokyo.

Hokusai has pictured the Tōkaidō in his prints—the villages and the mountains, the plains and the sea, the peasants and the pilgrims, the *rōnin* and the priests. He did add his immortal overlay to the tradition of the highway's immortality, but even the great Hokusai could only be an incident in the spread of its renown. The Tōkaidō's personality was no less haughty and arrogant long centuries before the artist. It was built by the gods, as everyone knows, and not by man. This may be the reason why it has fallen upon hard days in these modern times, now that the race of man has assumed the task of relieving the weary gods of so many of their duties. Axes have cut down the cryptomerias for miles because the trees interfered with telegraph wires. Furthermore, a new highway has now been built between the capitals, a road of steel. For most of the way this new road follows alongside the old, although sometimes departing in a straighter line. The vaulting arrogance of all was when man took the name "Tōkaidō" for a railway. The trains pass by the ancient shrines of the wayside with no tarrying for moments of contemplation. To-day a *samurai*, with a newspaper under one arm and a lunch box under the other—his two swords have been thus displaced—goes from Kyoto to Tokyo in as few hours as were the days of his father's journeying.

When the feudal emperors made this pilgrimage they were carried in silk-hung, lacquered palanquins, and fierce-eyed, two-sworded retainers cleared the streets and sealed the houses so that no prying eyes might violate sacrosanctity. As for our pilgrimage we appreciated that we were not sacred emperors and that we were coming along without announcement. The inhabitants kept the sides of their houses open and stared out upon us. We felt free, discreetly, to return their glances from under the brims of our pith helmets, but occasionally this freedom felt a panicky restraint within itself to keep eyes on the road.

In the legend of her famous ride, Lady Godiva, I believe, had the houses sealed before her approach as did those deified Japanese emperors. We doubted, that early morning, whether the dwellers along the Tōkaidō, if they had been told Lady Godiva's tale, would have had appreciation for her chastely wishing not to be seen, except as a mystifying and whimsical eccentricity. To preserve a deity from mortal eyes—yes, that might have been conceded as a conventional necessity. But our surety grew after a short advance that if the fulfilling of a similar vow by a Japanese Lady Godiva should have its penance depending merely upon the absence of attire, she could ride her palfrey in the environs of Kyoto inconspicuously and without exciting comment. At least such costuming would be in local fashion the first one or two hours after sunrise.

A mile is a mile the first day, and we had had three or four miles in the silence which comes from the feeling that one is really off.

"It's a good morning for boiling out," remarked Alfred, by way of breaking the spell.

We were in a narrow valley walking head on into the sun. It was an excellent morning for boiling out.

I suggested that it was a good time to take the first rest. We found a spot in a temple garden up a flight of exceedingly steep stone steps. Usually to throw off one's pack is to achieve the supreme emotional satisfaction of laziness, but on this first essay we failed to relax. It was perhaps partly that we had not yet boiled out our Western restlessness among other poisons, but also there was to be counted in as opposed to the quietude of the garden a most unrestful suggestion contributed by a conspicuous sign written in English and nailed to a post. It read:

"Foreigners Visiting Must Dismount Horses and Not Ride Into Temple."

There are visitors in the East whose idea of sightseeing the heathen gods might not preclude their riding their horses up onto the lap of the bronze Buddha of Kamakura. But how the priest imagined that horses were to be urged up those stone steps was a mystery veiled from our understanding.

It even created a pride in our alien blood that we were a race thought to be capable of such magic.

The Tōkaidō winds through the city of Ōtsu. It enters proudly as the chief street but escapes between rows of mean houses, becoming as nearly a characterless lane as the Tōkaidō can anywhere be. The town is the chief port of Lake Biwa of the famed eight views, and it is just beyond this town that the upstart railway takes itself off, together with its cindery smoke, on a straighter line than the Tōkaidō. The highway bends to the south in a swinging circle and wanders along for many a quiet mile before the two meet again. At the angle of the parting of the old and the new we stopped at a rest house for a bottle of *ramune*. This beverage is a carbonated, chemically compounded lemonade. Its wide distribution does possess one merit. The bottles may often be used as a sort of guide book. Almost every little shop along the road has a few bottles cooling in a wooden bucket of water. Thus, if a stranger is walking from one town to another and if, as is inevitable, he has been unable to learn anything about distances along the way, he may at least judge that he is approximately half through his journey when the labels on the bottles change the address of their origin to that of the town which he is seeking.

The *ramune* which we had at Ōtsu was warm and the shop was stifling and the flies were sticky. My clinging flannel shirt was unbuttoned, my sleeves were rolled up, and I had tied a handkerchief about my head. We carried our bottles out to a low bench to escape the baked odors of the shop, and while we were sitting and sipping two Japanese gentlemen came down the road, looking very cool under their sun umbrellas and in their immaculate *kimono*. Orthodox ambition in the temperate zone aims for respectability, power, and property, but in the tropics any temporary struggle, whether in war or trade, has as its lure the reward of a long, aristocratic, cooling calm. Our Japanese gentlemen, superiorly aloof to the perspiring world, appeared to be amusedly observing the habits and customs of the foreigner as exhibited by us. Their staring rankled. Until then I had been happy in the exact condition of my perspiration. Their observance now chilled the beads on my back. Any number of coolies could have come and stared, and called us brother—for all of that—but we were being made to realize suddenly that in the Orient the lower the blood temperature the higher the caste mark. The parent germ of all convention in the world is "not to lose face." It has been most highly developed by the Chinese and the Anglo-Saxon. For the Chinese it is personal, but it makes the renegade Anglo-Saxon, despite himself, keep on trying to hold up his chin in a blind call of blood loyalty to his own mob when facing the Asiatic.

We picked up our packs and started off. It was either to retire or nihilistically to hurl the packs at their immaculateness. Just as we began to move one of them said: "Do you speak English?"

The truth must be told that we recanted much of our wrath after the friendliness of a half-hour's roadside palaver. The meeting, however, had a uniqueness of experience far beyond anything merely casual. It allowed us the extraordinary record that we once did acquire local information from a Japanese whose conception of daily time and highroad space had some coincidence with our Western science of absolute fact. Mr. Yoshida, he who had called after us, knew that corner of Japan and he told us about it.

Alfred says: "Certain Japanese inexplicabilities are extremely ubiquitous." He thus confines himself to six words. I cannot. I require a paragraph. Despite the ubiquitous mystery, there is always one certainty: Whatever may be the thought processes of the Japanese concerning hours, distances, and direction, the inquirer may be sure of this: the answer will not be concerned with answering the question. The courteous answerer earnestly uses his judgment to determine what reply is likely to be most pleasing. If you appear weary, or in a hurry, then the distance to go is never very long. If you appear to be enjoying your walk, then the distance is a long way. The village which has been declared just around the bend of the road may be two *ri* off. This is the desire to please, inculcated by the *bushidō* creed of honorable conduct. It may be thought that such paradoxical solicitude becomes extremely irritating, but rarely does it. The wish to help is real, at least, and is not merely the carelessness of superficiality. The peasant may tell you that you have but a step to go, but if you are lost he will turn aside from his own path and show you the way, though it be for miles.

We noted down Mr. Yoshida's details concerning the inns and villages which we should find along the way to distant Nagoya. Experience soon told us to hold fast to his information, no matter the contradictions that were agreeably offered in its stead.

We shouldered our packs and again were off. After a time Alfred said: "I met Mr. Yoshida once at a dinner in America."

"Why didn't you tell him so?" I gasped.

Alfred seemed surprised at my amazement. As nearly as I could determine he must have completely disassociated the metabolic Alfred sitting on the bench in front of the rest house, drinking warm *ramune,* and the Alfred of practical America. Perhaps the Japanese believe in the "unfathomable mystery of the American mind."

We had six hours through the hills ahead of us if we were to keep on that night to Minakuchi. Our mentor had told us that one of the most luxurious of all the country inns in Japan was sequestered there. To hurry to any particular place was against our code, but this time it seemed reasonable to make an honorable exception.

The sun went down behind the paddy fields. The muddy waters of the terraces caught the gleaming yellows and reds, but our backs were against this suffusion of color. Into the darkness ahead the narrow road led on and on. Says the essayist: "The artist should know hunger and want." But surely not the art patron. He cannot perform his function of appreciation unless comfortably removed from immediate pangs. If I were to be an enthusiast over that wonderful sunset—as Alfred persisted in suggesting—I needed food. It had been fifteen hours since our cold breakfast and I thought of the inn with an ardency of vision.

When we did see the town it sprang up abruptly out of the fields. All along the streets the lights were shining through the paper walls. We made inquiry for the *yadoya* and in a moment were surrounded by volunteer guides. They are always diverting, the Japanese children, running along on their wooden clogs and looking up into your face.

Maids without number came running to the entrance of that aristocratic inn, and dropped to their knees. They bowed until their glossy black hair touched the ground. The auguries all appeared auspicious. Then came the mistress. There were many polite words, but no one took our rucksacks and no one invited us in. Every second's waiting for the bath and dinner was very, very long.

My Japanese of twelve years before had been but a few words. Days on the Trans-Siberian of grammar and dictionary study had not even brought back that little, but now suddenly I began to understand what the mistress of that inn was saying. I had no vanity in my understanding. The understanding was that we were not wanted. I had been tired and I had been hungry when we reached the door, but now I knew the unutterable weariness of smelling a dinner which may not be eaten.

The crowd was amused, but it showed its amusement considerately and with restraint. Nevertheless two *seiyō-jin* had lost face. Apparently the mistress did not wish such suspicious-looking foreigners, grimy, dustless, and coatless, to remain even in the same town. She called two *rikisha*. She named the next village. She had this much magnanimity that she purposed giving us the chance of orderly retreat.

I tried to continue smiling with dignity and affability. It is somewhat of a strain on diplomatic smiles when the subject of discussion is vitally concerned with one's own starvation. Nevertheless I did smile. I explained that whatever we did we were not going on to the next town. I knew the word for "another," and the word for "inn," and how to say, "Is it?" And thus I asked: "Another inn here, is it?" There was little incitement to believe that she understood except that her mouth pouted ever so slightly as if in surprise that I should imply that the mistress of such a superior inn could have any knowledge concerning mere bourgeois caravansaries.

Alfred, during this parleying, had put on his coat and in other subtle ways had transformed himself into a conventional foreigner. After that he had settled into repose and silence. I looked at him. I searched for a flaw. I declared by the great Tōkaidō itself that with such a fright-producing handicap as his ultra-Occidental beard we should never find resting spots outside the local jails.

"Humph!" he said. "Stop talking for a minute and put on your coat."

I succumbed. "All right, then," I said. "Here's for the magic of that vestment of respectability."

I sat down on the ground and untied the bag. The prophecy of magic was too feeble by far for the prestidigitation which followed. I shook out the folds of the garment which is called a coat, a mere two sleeves, a back and a front and a few buttons. The circle came closer. But it was not the coat after all which caused our audience so graciously to begin giving back our lost faces to us—it was the supermagic of one leg of a pair of silk pajamas.

A black-eyed jackdaw, a trifle more daring in her curiosity than the others, discovered the hem of that garment tipping out from a corner of my pack. She gave it a jerk, and then another. Next she looked up with coaxing persuasion, suggesting encouragement to tug again.

Alfred had insisted that I have those pajamas made in Kyoto. He has theories about the necessity of silk pajamas. I never, even remotely, followed the dialectics of his reasons, but I must add to the credit side of such theorizings that pajamas are a most intriguing garment to pass around for the benefit of an inn courtyard crowd. The maid gave the next tug and out they came. Everybody reached forward a finger and a thumb to feel.

Between the time of the discovery of the silk pajamas and their repacking—I cold-heartedly refused to exhibit a putting of them on—we rose from nobodies to persons of importance in Minakuchi. Even the mistress hinted that she had mentally recounted her space for guests and had thought of a luxurious corner of amply sufficient dimensions to spread two beds. There was, of course, no sane reason why we should not, then and there, have taken advantage of this altered atmosphere, but for me the inn had lost its savor. Anyone who has ever had some similar twist of psychology will appreciate the inside of my irrationalism. Others will not or cannot. I moved over to the *rikisha*. Alfred remained lingering. He, too, had noted the change in the mistress's attitude.

"How about making one more overture?" he suggested.

"Perhaps so," I answered, "but don't you feel that any experience which this inn might now hold for us would be an anti-climax after our present dramatic triumph?"

Alfred regretfully sniffed the fragrant steam drifting from the kitchen braziers.

"No, I decidedly don't feel so," he said, "but of course, if I have to save your dilettante soul from anti-climaxes, I suppose I can sleep in a rice field—but whatever you do, do it!"

I threw our bags into the *rikisha* and we climbed in after them, and were off to the other inn.

We made our impact against this objective much more catapultic. There was nothing tentative in our kicking off our shoes and getting well under the lintel before any mistress of authority could appear. Our onslaught paralysed the advance line of receiving maidens, and we settled down on the interior mats and assumed a contemplative calm. We continued to sit thus oblivious to the excitement heaped upon excitement. We were islands of fact in the midst of an ocean of conversation. After the ocean had dried up because none had words left, we were still obviously remaining, and there was nothing left to do but to make the best of us. A maid picked up our bags and bowed very low. She retreated toward the inner darkness and we followed, first along a corridor and then up a flight of railless stairs to a room open on two sides against a courtyard garden.

To have been in harmony at all with the ancient traditions of the Tōkaidō, coolies should have been carrying our luggage in huge red and gold lacquered chests. The room to which we were taken would have been a room of dignity even for a *daimyō*. The maid placed our two dusty Occidental rucksacks on the shelf under the *kakemono*. Their very presence piped a chanty that our possessing that room was ironic comedy. We began to laugh. A *nee-san* is as ever ready to laugh as water is to flow, and with no other grand cause than just the doing. Our maid began laughing with us, and up the stairs came all the other maids in curiosity. Ensconced, their interest seemed permanent. Our vocabulary was very far from being sufficient to protect our Western prudery. As a last resort we took them by their shoulders and turned them around and urged them in this unsubtle manner from the door.

I began undressing at one end of the room, leaving my garments in my wake as I rolled over the soft matting. When I reached the *kakemona* shelf, I slipped into my silk pajamas. When we went below to find the honorable bath we at least left the room looking not so bare as our meagre luggage had predicted.

We returned from the bath and banked our cushions on the narrow balcony overhanging the garden. A slight breeze stirred the branches of the trees and started swinging the paper lanterns which hung over a stone fountain. Other guests of the inn had finished their dinners and it was their toothbrush hour. Dressed in their cotton *yukata* they stood bending over shining brass basins filled from the well fountain. It would probably be useless to ask any Occidental to imagine that the function of teeth cleansing with long, flexible handled brushes may be a social and picturesque

13

addendum to garden life. We have too long looked upon ablutions as being merely necessitous.

Dinner came. Whether strict philosophical truth lies in the belief that every sensation is unique, or whether in the contrary that no experience can be other than a repetition of some situation which has been staged over and over again in the turning of the cosmic wheel, I shall continue to maintain that a wanderer who has gone from half after four in the morning, fortified only by a mouthful of cold breakfast, until nine at night, and has walked something more than twenty-five miles under a hot sun, and has had one dinner snatched away from him, and then finds himself risen from a bath and sitting in the slow, warm, evening air in a room of simple harmony, and then a small lacquer table is placed before him with the alluring odors of five steaming dishes ascending to his nose—yes, I shall continue to maintain that such a wanderer has a human right to protest that such a situation is an event.

They replenished the tables with second supplies of the first dishes and with first and second dishes of new courses. We had two kinds of soup and three varieties of fish. We had chicken and we had vegetables and boiled seaweed. And we finished with innumerable bowls of rice. At the end they brought iced water and tea and renewed the charcoal in the braziers for our smoking. The tobacco clouds drifted from our lips. Only one possible thought was worth putting into words and that was the request to have the beds laid. However, the evening was destined not for such sensuous oblivion.

Breaking in upon this godly languor came a visitation by the entire family of the inn. The family particularly embraced in its intimacy also the maid-servants and the men-servants. Even the baby had been wakened to come. In the beginning Alfred offered cigarettes in lieu of conversation and I thumbed the dictionary for compliments for the baby. The blue-bound book of phrases proved to be rich in fitting adjectives, and my efforts were rewarded with sufficient approval to encourage us to go on with a search for compliments for mother and father and all the others. The baby crawled forward inch by inch until one of the strange foreign giants courageously picked it up. Our guests had first sat in a very formal half-circle, but under the expansiveness of growing goodwill the line was breaking.

It was a night, however, of many visitations. Hardly had we, as hosts, with the aid of the baby, carried the attack with some success against rigid self-consciousness when there came the sound of a step on the stair. Immediately the mood of laughter changed to one of marked quietness and expectancy. The circle readjusted itself. The mother snatched back the baby and by some technique ended its expressions of curiosity and reduced it, as only a Japanese baby can be reduced, to a pair of staring eyes. We sat waiting the coming of the intruder. The *nee-sans* bowed their heads to the floor.

The awaited one was a tall young man, with round, pinkish, glistening limbs, and a round face. He dropped heavily to his knees and bent over until his forehead touched the mat, continuing this salutation for some time. Then he sat up smiling and satisfied. He had brought with him three or four foreign books and he was, without need of introduction, the village scholar, Minakuchi's representative of modernity, a precious and honored cabinet of wisdom newly come home from the University. After his smiling expansion he next composed his features to solemnity. He adjusted his *yukata* taut over his knees. Then he waited until the last quiver in his audience succumbed into the extreme quietude of painful tension. Even the breeze lulled. He spoke:

"I—am—in—this—room!"

The heads of the circle nodded and renodded to each other. What had the foreigners to answer to that?

We tried to express a proper appreciation.

"It—is—cold—today—but—it—was—raining—yesterday."

An opinion about temperature is more or less a personal judgment, but the falling of raindrops is a material fact. On the yesterday it had not rained.

This time the circle could not restrain itself but sighed with positive and audible contentment. Minakuchi had been vindicated. If the audience showed content with its spokesman, it was as nothing compared to his own contentment. The artist in tongues now opened his books with a business-like air and put on his spectacles. His visit was not, then, purely social. The sentences which followed were, as nearly as we could determine, questions to us. They came, a word at a time, out of his dictionary. The conventions of speech which the Japanese employ in polite inquiry have been molded by symbolism, mysticism, and analogy into phrases most remote from the original rudiment. A word by word translation into English carries no meaning whatsoever. We answered by: "Oh, yes, yes,—of course."

15

The baby was growing restless. The scholar took in this sign from the corner of his eye. His dramatic sense was keen. He had no intention that his audience should become bored and he snapped shut the books with the pronounced meaning that everything had been settled as far as he was concerned. Then he clapped his hands loudly. Instantly from below came more footsteps and a clank-clanking of metal on wood, and in a moment into the room walked an officer of the police. His heavy dress uniform was white, with gold braid twisting round and about the sleeves and shoulders. His sword, the secret of the rhythmic clanking, was almost as tall as himself. He faced us rigidly and without a smile, then slowly sank to his knees and dropped his head to the mat. I have faith that that man, without an extra heart-beat, would have joined a sure death charge across a battlefield, but his present duty brought the red blush of painful embarrassment to his olive skin from the edge of his tight collar to the fringe of his black hair. He was silently and perspiringly suffering in the cause of duty—but what was his duty?

I do not know just how we gained the idea, if it were not through telepathy, but we decided that he was discounting the abilities of the interpreter down to an extreme minimum, although he listened attentively enough to some long statement. After the explanation, which seemingly concerned us, the youth arose and with much dignity withdrew from the room followed by many expressions of appreciation from the inn family. Every one of us who had been left behind, except the baby who had gone to sleep, now waited for some continuance of the drama, but nothing proceeded to materialize. I grew so sleepy that if the policeman had suddenly said that we were to be executed at sunrise the most interesting part of the information would have been the finding out whether we could sleep until that hour. As I did not know how polite it might be to say that *we* were tired, I found a phrase, "*You* must be very tired," to which I linked, "therefore *we* shall go to bed."

This veiled ultimatum was as graciously accepted as if they had been waiting those exact words to free them to go their way. The *nee-sans* ran for mattresses and prepared the beds. Then they hung the great mosquito netting. After that we all said our good-nights, all except the police official who, image like, remained sitting against the wall.

By earnest beseeching we had persuaded the maids not to close the wooden *shōji* around the balcony. Thus, when we turned out the lamp and stretched out on our beds, the starlight came in. It shone on the white uniform. I had never happened to have the experience of going to sleep under the eye of a policeman but realism proved that practice was unnecessary. Sinking to oblivion was as positive as a plunge. The vast embracing fluid of rest closed in over my head.

I was dreamless until I awoke under a sudden, crushing nightmare. I thought that an army of white and gold uniforms had mobilized and was tramping over my chest, taking care that every heel should fall pitilessly. The one policeman who existed in reality had been trying to wake me up and he had evidently had a task, but as soon as he was sure that my eyes were open to stay he forwent further assault. He had lighted the lamp and I could see behind him a naked coolie, convulsively gasping for breath. The man was carrying an envelope. The officer took the envelope and then sent him off. He reeled to the stairs holding his panting sides. The officer then took out a sheet of paper and handed it to me. The page was written in modified English but was quite intelligible. While the sentences were nothing more than a series of questions, at the same time they gave a clue to the mystery of the evening.

Our inn-keeper had had the inspiration to call upon the scholar-interpreter to ask us the questions which all travellers must answer for the police record in every town where a stop is made for the night. We had been correct about there being one doubter in Minakuchi of the ability of the interpreter. In a plot for his own amusement the police officer had sent a runner to a neighboring town to have the conventional list of questions translated into English, and thus to compare our written answers with the answers given him by the youth. There they were, the questions: who were we—how old—profession—antecedents whence and whither. If one is tempted into wayward rebellion against such minuteness of interrogation, it is wise to remember that the claim of a sense of humor may be considered very poor testimony in a Japanese court perchance misunderstandings at any time arise and the answers in the police records have to be looked up.

I wrote out the answers. With no one in the room as a witness except ourselves, the officer allowed a twinkle to come into his eye. He even winked and pointed to where the youth had sat. Then he shut up the paper in his register and blew out the light and clanked off down the stairs. Again we slept.

The etiquette of an inn is that all crude appearance of hurry should be avoided by waiting in one's room in the morning for one's bill. The Japanese do not travel hurriedly; if they wish an early start they get up in time. We had asked for an early breakfast and it had been served at the hour which we had named. We had happened to have good intentions about not rushing. Nevertheless, of course, we fell into an inevitable hurry. After breakfast I had been so interested in sitting on our balcony watching the waking up of the day that I forgot to pack my rucksack. Alfred said that he would pay the bill downstairs and wait at the door.

When I arrived under the lintel where we had left our shoes I felt as if I were intruding. The bearded foreigner was surrounded by the inn family and each member was handing him a present. There were blue and white Japanese towels folded into decorated envelopes, and there were fans and postcards. The cost of the gift fans may have been little but the maker had taken his designs from models of the best tradition, and the fans to be found for sale are not comparable.

The daughters of the house walked with us until we came to the Tōkaidō and then they pointed out our direction and stood waving farewells until we could see them no longer. I waited until then before making inquiry about the amount of the bill. This detail was a matter of distinct importance. When we met in Kyoto we pooled our purses and the common fund was entrusted to Alfred's care. Neither of us had made much effort to acquire theoretical information about what daily expenses might be. We had just so much paint with which to cover the surface of the definite number of days before our steamer would carry us away, and this meant that we would have to mix thick or thin accordingly. Experience only could teach us what items we could afford and what bargains we should have to make. I thus awaited the answer about the bill with flattering attention.

"The bill, including extras for iced water and cigarettes and getting our special dinner after every one else had finished," said the treasurer with appropriate solemnity, "was three *yen*." (A *yen* is about fifty cents.) "And," he concluded, "I gave a full *yen* for the tea-money tip."

We waited until we sat down for the first rest before we attempted a practical financial forecast. We divided the number of remaining days into the sum of the paper notes carried in a linen envelope. The answer quieted our fears and exceeded our hopes. Putting aside a reserve for extra occasions, beyond our inn bills we would be able to afford the luxury of spending along the road twenty-five cents a day for tea, tobacco, and chemical lemonade.

There is something unnatural in such simplicity of finance, as anyone must agree who believes at all in the jealousy of the gods. I should have been forewarned by an old Chinese tale that I had been told only a fortnight before. It was while sitting in a Beijing restaurant. The teller was a most revolutionary son of a most conservative mandarin. A peasant once entertained a god unawares. In the morning the god told the peasant that any wish which he might name would be granted, be it for riches, or power, or even the most beautiful maid in all the dragon kingdom to be his wife. But the peasant asked that he might only be assured that until the end of his days he need never doubt when hungry that he would have food, and at the fall of night that he would find a pillow on which to lay his head. The god looked at him sorrowfully and said: "Alas! You have asked the impossible. Such favors are reserved for the gods alone."

We got up from our figuring blithely, indulging ourselves in the idea that we could achieve such evenness of expenditure. Think what an upsetting of ponderous economics and competitive jungle law there would be if the world could and should abruptly take any such consideration of its wealth!

The payer of the bill had also added that he had given a full *yen* for the tea-money tip. In those large areas of Japan where the barbarous foreigner has not yet intruded with his indiscriminate giving, there is to be found the ancient system of tea-money. The tea-money custom is founded on the belief that the wayfarer is the personal guest of the host. When the guest departs he is not paying a bill, he is making a present, and to this sum he adds from a quarter to a third part extra. This extra payment is the tea-money and is to be divided by the host among the servants. The departing guest is then given a present. All in all, leave taking is a function.

A guest does not ask nor demand. He offers a request and thereby confers a supreme favor upon any servant fortunate enough to be designated. All this pleasant service has not the embarrassment that one must confine a request to any particular maid so as to escape the necessity of widespread tipping at departure. It is all in the tea-money.

The Furnace of Hades

A very famous book in Japan is named the "*Kojiki*," and the word means "A Record of Ancient Matters." We thought on our second morning as we walked through the hills that if there should happen to be a modern chronologist recording a present-time *Kojiki* those hours of the sun's approaching meridian would be entered without dispute as The-Forever-Famous-Never-To-Be-Equalled-Day-Of-Fire. In the valleys there was no breeze; on the summits there was no shade; and everywhere it seemed probable that on the next instant the road would blister into molten heat bubbles under our feet. However—to anticipate—if such a postulated chronicler had so styled that second day of our walking as one without chance of peer among historical days of heat, on the very next following day he would have had to turn back to cross out his lines. In the burning glare of the rice fields, anything that had gone before was so easily surpassed that we forever lost belief in maximums, unless indeed kinetic energy might continue on such a wild rampage of vibration that it would shake itself completely out of existence.

Our first rest of the second day, as I said, was devoted to the arithmetic of finance. At that early hour the dew was not yet off the grass, but when we began planning for another rest the world had grown parched. Looking about for some possible spot we saw through the trees the roof of a small temple. We halted at the entrance and tried to push open the gate. It would not move. It was nailed to the ribs of the fence, but the gate was low enough to be vaulted. Our feet fell on the ghost of a path that had once led to the shrine. Harsh brambles and weeds had fought for the possession of the path until they had almost conquered the flaggings. If we thought at all we thought that that particular walk must have been abandoned for some other entrance and as the scratches were not very serious we pushed our way through until at last we stepped forth into the temple yard. Not a sign of caretaking devotion was anywhere in evidence nor was there a nodding priest sitting in the temple door.

Sometimes the Chinese desert their temples but, when incense is no longer burned before an altar, celestial practical sense leaves little that is movable behind. We slowly walked up the steps to the door, expecting to find the temple rifled. The door was sealed by spiders' webs. We then walked around the balcony and peered through the wide cracks in the *shōji*. No fingers of man had rummaged there since the priests had said the last mass, but the fingers of decay had been busily working. The rotted fabrics hung down from the altars of the shrines and the ashes of the incense in the bronze bowls was hidden by the blacker dust which the wind had carried through the shutters. Surely we were the first intruders to step upon the balcony since the gate had been swung to and nailed.

We walked around the corners until we had seen everything that there was to see and then we jumped down to a grassy slope on the shady side of the temple and stretched ourselves out in relaxation. It was very quiet. As I knew Alfred could sleep for ten minutes and then wake up to the instant, I closed one eye and then the other. They both came open together. I had felt a soft dragging across my ankles and I raised my head to see a very thin, long, green and grey snake raising its head up between my feet to stare into my face. After a beady inspection it wriggled away with slow undulations into the grass. And then, from the spot where that snake had taken passage over my ankles, came the head of another. I jerked my feet up under me.

The instant before there had been an oppressive quietness. The silence had been so supreme that we ourselves had scarcely spoken. Now there was a vast hurrying of little noises. Lizards ran along the rafters under the roof and dropped down the wall, as lizards do, to flatten themselves away into corners. Huge buzzing flies rose from the surface of the pond and bumped against us aimlessly. Mosquitoes came from the shadows. I had thrown my helmet on the grass. I picked it up to find it beset with ants. I tried to beat them out of the lining by pounding the hat against the side of the temple. The effort broke loose a roach infested board.

We grinned at each other a little shamefacedly when we were safely out into the sunshine of the highroad. We had not stayed to argue in the temple yard. As we stood thus vanquished and ejected, two peasants came passing by. They looked at us, then glanced hurriedly at the temple roof above the low trees, and then eyed us again. They mumbled a word or two. Perhaps they were trying to tell us that an accursed goblin had taken over their shrine to be the abode of insects and crawling things. I was not so sure that I had not seen the glowing eyes of a goblin staring malevolently at us from the cracks of the *shōji* when I turned to look back over my shoulder as we fled.

For a long way my blood welcomed the sun. The road led down into a broad valley to become later little more than an interminable bridge across the terraced paddy fields. The rice had sprouted but had not grown rank enough to block the mirror surface of the water from throwing back the heat rays. Ahead were low-lying hills with higher slopes beyond and from the map we thought that over that barrier would be the broad plain across which we would find the road leading straight to Nagoya.

There was one ambition to luxury which we always possessed—when we chose a rest spot we wished one of comfort and, if it could be included, also that it should have a view. Curiously, owners of land do not seem to endeavour to provide such rest places for sensitive travellers, at least to be obtrusive at any exact second when desired. We had taken seven or eight miles across the valley at an unusually accelerated pace since our last attempt at a rest. Messages from the cords of our legs were telling us to concede some compromise to our particularity. However, we continued walking and searching without paying attention to the messages. The grass patches always disclosed little ant hills upon close inspection and the occasional heaps of stones to be found were never under the shade. That obstinacy of ours was of the stuff ambition should be, and finally its persistency met due reward. We found a wide, shady platform built against a long building, half house, half granary. The building flanked the road at a bend and as we made the turn we could see the family of the house lying on the floor. An old man was telling an elaborate story and his listeners were so intent upon the tale that none of them happened to look up to see us. The platform was out of their vision and we thought that we might rest there with the comfortable feeling that trespassing does not exist unless discovered.

The tale that was being told was undoubtedly humorous. The daughters of the family were hard struggling with laughter. The men were emphasizing their approval by pounding on the rim of the charcoal brazier with their iron pipes. All were repeating a continuous *hai, hai*. But there was a baby, and the baby was not so much interested in the story as he was in a butterfly. He suddenly betook himself to his dimpled legs and circled into the road in pursuit. The whims of the gyrations of the mighty hunter carried him to a spot where the next turn left him facing two foreigners on the platform. He stood with feet apart and carefully lifted the corner of his diminutive shirt to his mouth for more careful cogitation, as any Japanese child should and does do when confronted by a kink in the well-ordered running of affairs.

The mother called out an admonition but there was no response from the *akanbō*. She left the story to find out what might be the enchantment. She, too, began staring without responding to admonitions. Another head bobbed around the corner post and then another and another until finally the teller of the tale himself forsook the realm of fancy for fact and followed after his audience. We said "*O-hayō!*"—which is good-morning—and they said "*O-hayō!*" After that their rigid attention included everything from our hats to our boots. Then in a body they walked back into the house and were quiet except for the most hushed of whispers.

"Two trespassing strangers are about to receive some mark of respect," said Alfred.

"Respect of being told to move on, most likely," was my more worldly judgment.

"How about betting a foreign dinner to be paid in Yokohama before the boat sails?" asked Alfred.

I took the wager, and lost.

The old man who had been the teller of the story now reappeared. He was somewhat embarrassed but at each step of his approach he had a still broader smile. He was short and he was thin, with lean, knotted muscles. His limbs had grown clumsy from heavy toil. His face was squat as if in his malleable infancy some evil hand had pressed his forehead down against his chin. One piece of cloth saved him from nudity. He was a coolie of generations of coolies, but despite his embarrassment and despite his clumsy limbs, the very spirit of graciousness created a certain grace as he placed a tray before us. He backed away with low bow succeeding low bow. The tray held a pot of tea and two cups and some thin rice cakes.

Good man, he fortunately never knew what an argument his gift precipitated! My opponent began it all by suggesting that we leave a twenty *sen* silver piece on the tray. I disputed.

"A cup of tea is of such slight cost to the giver," was my eloquent and disputatious argument, "that by being of no price it becomes priceless and thus is a perfect symbol of a complete gift in an imperfect world. Japan has this tradition which we have lost in our own civilization. This simplicity allows the poorest and humblest to give a gift to the richest and mightiest in the purity of hospitality. If we leave money on the tray we are robbing the peasant of his privilege."

Alfred would have none of my transcendentalism. "By leaving money," he said, "a sum which means no more to us than does the cup of tea to the peasant, we are making an exchange of gifts. We know that he is very poor. Twenty *sen* is probably more than the return for two days of his labour. It will buy him a pair of wooden *geta* or a new pipe, or a bamboo umbrella for his wife, or such a toy for the baby as it has never dreamed of. After giving our gift we shall disappear down the road, leaving the memory of two ugly but generous foreign devils."

There was no dispute between us about wishing to leave some gift. The final compromise was somewhat on my side as we gave a package of chocolate to the child. We carried the chocolate for emergency's sake and it had cost several times twenty *sen*. I do not believe that Japanese children like chocolate and there was more than a possibility that this highly condensed brand would make the baby ill. Surely the deposed gods of the ancient Tōkaidō must have made merry if the news of our analytics was carried to their Valhalla. Nevertheless our present, wrapped in a square of white paper according to the etiquette of gifts, was received by the family with as many protestations of appreciation as if we had handed them a deed to perpetual prosperity.

The rays of the forenoon's sun when we were crossing the valley of the rice fields had sent up heat waves from the dust of the road until the road itself seemed to me to have a quaking pitch and roll. We were now in the full glory of the noontide. I was becoming somewhat disturbed over certain phenomena. Trees and rocks and houses fell into the dance of the heat waves with an undignified stagger. Sometimes the bushy trees reeled away in twos and threes where but a moment before I had seen but one. The most disconcerting part of the development was my peculiar impersonal interest and study of my own distress. I knew that my eyes were aching and I knew that the trees were really standing still. I had the perfect duality of being fascinated by the day and thus not wishing to be any place else in the world and yet, as I said, of being extremely disturbed by the preliminary overtures of a sunstroke. We had had about two hours of climbing since we left the house of the rice farmer and we were on the summit of the last high hills. Immediately ahead the rocky path dropped sharply down into the plain. A rest-house marked the point where the climbing changed to the descent. I suggested a halt.

The rest-house was more than a peasant's hut. It was easy to believe that in more aristocratic days it had been an inn of some pretension. Now it was a spot for weary coolies to throw down their heavy packs for a few minutes' rest in its shade by day or by night to curl up on the worn mats. We walked into the deepest recess of the entrance before we sat down. I could look beyond a half-folded screen into the kitchen. The polished copper pots and the iron and bronze bowls were not of this generation. Probably tomorrow's will find them on a museum shelf or cherished in some antique shop. However, I had no desire to discover curios nor did I have any preference whether the inn was old or new, nor whether it had been its fortune to entertain *daimyō* or pariahs. We first asked for something to drink. The hostess dragged up a bucket from the well and brought us bottles of *ramune* which had been cooling in the depths. I drank the carbonated stuff and then pushed my rucksack back along the mat for a pillow and closed my eyes for a half-hour's blissful forgetfulness. When I awoke the throbbing under my eyelids had passed away and for the first time I really looked at our hostess. She was kneeling beside us and was slowly fanning our faces.

Her teeth were painted black, as was once the fashion for married women. She had known both toil and poverty, but it was not a peasant's face into which I looked. Her thin fingers and wasted forearms found repose in the lines which the ancient artists were wont to copy from the grace of Old Japan. Her calm face was beautiful.

It was time that we should make our way down the rocky path. She brought us tea before we went. The bill for everything, as I remember, was about seven cents. We left a silver coin beside the teapot. She began to tell us that we had made a mistake. We told her no. Shielded by an unworldly, intangible delicacy, I doubt whether any rudeness of her guests ever became sufficiently real to her to disturb her passivity or her emotions, but such a guardianship presents a thin callous against sympathy. As we said goodbye a sudden sense of human mutuality smote the three of us, an experience of sheer bridging-over intuition which sometimes comes for a second.

The absolute relaxation had so marvellously driven out the devils from my eyes that I did not even tell Alfred of my hallucinations. To make up for our lingering we pushed on through the villages without stopping to wander into temple grounds or to explore by-ways. Between a misreckoning of miles on our part and some misinformation which I gathered from a peasant, we reached the rather large town of Shiki an hour earlier than we had hoped. As we strolled through the main street, we saw several inns which might well have given us comfortable shelter, but I sensed that the traveller at my side was waiting for some bubbling of inspiration. I kept silent, an expiation for having carried a disproportionate number of points that day. We continued walking. I could see the fringe of the first rice field ahead. My faith was beginning to waver but before I erred by showing it Alfred stopped abruptly and inquired the Japanese word for inn. He then asked for one or two other words and adjectives. Thus armed he stepped into a shop, the appearance of which had perhaps been the stimulus to his inspiration.

The shop had glass windows and a glass door. It was the most metropolitan example of commercial progressiveness which we had seen since we left Kyoto. In fact, compared to the other shops of Shiki it had as haughty an exclusiveness as any portal along New Bond Street seeks to maintain over possible rivals. Looking through the glass of the door we discovered that the floor was not covered with matting. Such a last touch of foreignism meant that one could walk in without taking off one's dusty boots. I do not remember that we ever again found this detail of Western culture outside the port cities. In the heart of the most isolated mountain range the most lonesome charcoal burner knows three things about the foreigner: that he is hairy like the red fox; that he has a curious and barbarous custom known as kissing; that his boots are part of his feet.

Into this shop, then, Alfred walked without having to undo his bootlaces. There was also an aristocratic glass counter and under the glass, in show trays, were gold watches. Behind this counter sat a young man in a *kimono* of black silk. His face was pale, ascetic, and contemplative. He smiled and bowed in formal hospitality. The grace of such a bow comes from centuries of saying *yes* instead of *no*. A cultured Japanese, almost any Japanese, never flatly contradicts unless to deny another's self-derogatory statement. The *iie* (used as "no") is rarely heard and the carrying over of the omnibus *hai, hai,* or the more polite *sayō,* into the English *yes* often brings consternation to the Westerner seeking accurate information.

Alfred said, "Please, good inn" (directly translated). As if the pale and ascetic seller of gold watches was accustomed daily to having perspiring foreigners with packs on their backs inquire for this information, he bowed again and smiled and said, "*hai, hai!*" This time the *hai, hai* did mean yes. He drew his *kimono* tighter about his hips and adjusted his silken *obi,* and walked out of the shop with us. Apologizing for the necessity of going before, he piloted us through turns of the street to the gateway of an inn. Calling for the mistress he made a dignified oration of introduction, and backed away from our sight with innumerable appreciations for the honor of being asked to be of service.

The Miles of the Rice Plains

The experiences of the second of our Japanese Nights' Entertainments were as impersonal, as far as the inn's paying special attention to us was concerned, as the first evening's had not been. The police record was brought to us with an English translation of the questions and we wrote the answers without complication. The incidents which may develop in one inn quite naturally have a wide variation from the happenings which may arise in another, but the general machinery of hospitality differs but little. There is, in fact, far less contrast in the essentials of comfort between the ordinary provincial inn and the native hotels of the first order in Tokyo or Kyoto than there is to be found in a like comparison of hotels in our civilization. It might even be said that the simple and fundamental artistry of the shelter which houses the peasant in Japan has in its possession the root forms of the taste which charms the homes of the cultured.

Immediately after we had applied ourselves to the police record and had had our steaming hot bath, a *nee-san* brought the small dinner tables. If ever this particular maid had enjoyed the frivolity of laughter for laughter's sake, she had long since banished any such promotion of irresponsible dimples from the corners of her mouth, although it should be stated that she was far from having arrived at an age to provoke a solemn and serious outlook upon life. Her eyes wandered up to the ceiling and around the edges. She was bored. Furthermore she appeared distressed at having to witness the table errors of ignorant foreigners. We insulted the honorable rice by heaping sugar upon it and we drank cold water when we should have sipped tea. We asked for a few extras to the menu. She repeated over our words, caught in amazement that we could change the barking sounds through which we found communication with each other into the music of Japanese speech. We asked if she were not afraid of barbarous foreigners, but she rather contemptuously rejoined that she could see no reason for being afraid in the shelter of her own inn. I then concocted from the dictionary an elaborate sentence which asked whether her expectation of how fearsome a foreigner might be was excelled by the examples in flesh and blood before her. The truth of her obvious conviction and the sense of required politeness of hospitality struggled each for utterance with such disconcerting effect that she used her turned-in toes to patter away down the flight of stairs and we saw our disapprover not again until she came to spread the beds.

We had planned to explore the shops of Shiki by lantern light after dinner but the two beds so aggressively allured us that we never stepped over them. The coverings were the usual heavy quilts buttoned into sheets. Such a combination coverlet is generally long enough for the foreign sleeper as the Japanese habit on cold nights is to disappear completely under the layer, but at the inn in Shiki for some reason the length was decidedly curtailed and the mattresses were correspondingly short. However, at the end of such a day of fire as we had had I was contemptuous of such limitations. I expected to sleep on the quilt and not under it.

For an hour, covered only by my cotton *yukata*, I knew the comfort of airy rest. Then I awoke to a sensation I had almost forgotten. I was chilled through. I entered upon a campaign of trying to get back to sleep by wrapping the abbreviated quilt about my shoulders. The far from satisfactory result was that my legs were left dangling in the chill drafts while the protected upper surfaces melted. Next I essayed a system of sliding the quilt up and down, executing retreats from too copious perspiration. This procedure met with some success but the required watchfulness was hardly a soporific. I called myself a tenderfoot. Some slight appreciation of how ridiculous it all was destroyed any high tragedy of self-sympathy but it could not keep me from loathing Alfred for breathing so tranquilly. Finally I got up, determined to force my ingenuity to find some balance between such excesses. Then I saw that Alfred's eyes were wide open.

I know not what the temperature of that room was in actual Fahrenheit degrees, but too many truth-tellers have secretly confided to me that they have found just such uncanny nights in Japan to disbelieve that the midnight "Hour of the Rat" has not at times a malignancy independent of mere thermometer readings. That night was neither cold nor hot; it was both and it was both at the same instant. My skin had been flushed to a mild fever from its long bath in the sun's rays, but the flesh beneath now grew iced when not swaddled beneath the furnace of the quilt. My inspiration, after sitting for a time and studying all the possible materials in the room, was to build a tent. I was so successful that I hurled a defiance at the "Hour of the Rat," and for another half-hour—perhaps it was—I again knew the positiveness of sleep.

The Japanese believe that they are a silent people. That faith is one of the supreme misbeliefs of the world. Before dinner, when we were sitting on our narrow balcony, we had said good-evening to a circle of young men who were lounging on cushions in the large room next to ours. Later they dressed and went out and we forgot them. I awoke to hear through the thin wall that they had returned. They were holding a Japanese conversation. Such a conversation can only be described by telling what it is not. In rhythm it is neither the cæsura of the French peasant woman retailing gossip, nor is it the eluding tempo-harmonic tune of the Red Indian drum beat. It is not the Chinese intoning, nor is it a staccato. At first the foreign ear does not distinguish the beat of the cadences but once captured the appreciation of the subtle metrical wave is never again lost. We had the opportunity of full orientation that night. The paper wall was but a second tympan to our ears.

Their conversation as an entity was a musical composition effected without counterpoint and played by the instruments in succession. First there was a swing of phrases from one speaker, and then after a decorous and proper dramatic pause there was an answering swing from another. No speaker was interrupted. The right of reply was passed about as if it were as physically tangible as a loving cup.

There was one distinct suggestion from the monotony of it all above every other impression, a something absolutely alien to any Occidental conversation. While they talked and drank tea and drank tea and talked, I twisted about under my tent puzzled to solve what that impression was. Suddenly I found words to express to myself the sought-for revelation. The effect of a long Japanese conversation is that of *voiceful contemplation*.

31

Separated from them physically only by a paper wall, we belonged to another world, a world which has ordered its existence without finding contemplation and its manifestations a necessary adjunct.

The mosquitoes, which all night had kept up a noisy circling over our net, flew off at daybreak. Some speaker spoke the concluding word in the next room and for a few minutes the universe was quiet. Then came the high shrieking of the ungreased axles of coolie carts being dragged to the rice fields. I took my quilt and cushions out onto the balcony. The inn began waking up. Down in the garden two kitchen maids appeared. They were arousing their energy by dipping their faces into brass basins of cold well water. I left my balcony and wandered below to find a basin for myself.

The inn had filled during the night with guests of all descriptions and ranks. They were coming forth from under their quilts. A *nee-san* stepped to the wellside and filled a basin for me and then ran off to find a gift toothbrush. Another maid, lazily binding on her *obi*, stayed her dressing for a moment to pour cool water from a wooden dipper over my head and neck. Getting up in the morning is a social cooperation in a Japanese inn.

Breakfast came. After breakfast I sat down on the balcony cushions to smoke and to breathe the delicious morning air and I promptly went to sleep. I wished to go on sleeping forever and to let the world work, or walk, or talk, or do anything it might choose to do, but Alfred appeared, saying that he had paid the bill. He had stuffed our presents into his rucksacks and had had the dramatic farewells to himself. After one has accepted a going-away present, one goes. Tense goodbyes do not brook recapture. The super-wanderer is thus forbidden ever to retrace his steps. For him alone, his life being always the anticipation of the next note of the magic flute, does the present become real by eternally existing as a becoming. He will not pay the price for contentment, which is to relive and rethink the past.

When we at length reached Nagoya, where the government bureau records temperatures scientifically, we learned that the week had been really one of extraordinary heat. Among other symptoms of the week, deranged livers and prickly irritation had inspired angry letters in the readers' columns of the foreign newspapers, belaboring everything native, particularly the casual discarding of clothing. A newspaper editor told us that such attacks of hyper-sensitiveness over nudity come not to foreigners newly arrived nor to those residents who sanely take long vacations back to their homelands (where they may have the rejuvenation of themselves being homogeneous with the masses), but to the conscientious unfortunates who remain too long at their posts. Round and about them for the twenty-four hours of the day and the seven days of the week surges the sea of native life. The feeling of lonesome strangeness, which can never be entirely lost by the foreigner, feeds on its own black moods and this poisonous diet suddenly nourishes a dull hatred. Then come the bitter letters to the press demanding that the Japanese reform themselves into Utopian perfection and threatening that unless they so do the foreign guests of the empire will assemble in convention and design an all-enveloping bag (with a drawing string to be pulled tight about the neck of the wearer) as a national costume for their hosts for evermore.

If hot days in the port cities, where there is some mild regulation of costume, can bring such disturbances of mind to anxiously missioning folk, we thought that it was as well that they were not walking with us that day through the villages of the broad plain which slopes from Mount Keisoku to Ise Bay. It was before we were out of the hills that our road carried us through a grove. A stone-flagged walk led into the shadows of the trees and we could see at its end the beginning of a long flight of stone steps which bespoke some hidden and ancient shrine beyond. A small stream flowed alongside the path and cut our road under an arched stone bridge. We heard shouts of laughter from the pines and the next moment an avalanche of children came tumbling along as fast as their legs could take them. Some were cupids with bright colored *yukata* streaming from their shoulders. Some did not have even that restraint. A tall, slender maiden was in pursuit, and the pursuit was part of some game. They dashed by us through the light and shadow and were lost again in the pines.

It was the reincarnation of a Greek relief. In that flash of the moment in which we saw them, the glistening nude body of the pursuing girl running through the green and brown and grey of the grove was passionately and superbly the plea of nature against man's crucifying purity upon the cross of sophistication.

I regretted to Alfred the having within me so much of that very sophistication that I had begun immediately to moralize upon such a sheerly beautiful vision. He, who had been saying nothing, replied with an end-all to the subject. "Your mild regret," he said, "that dispassionate analysis has displaced passionate creativeness is the penalty you pay for the pleasure of studying your own sadness."

The Greeks, I believe, had for one of their two axioms by which they covered the conduct of wise living, "No excess in anything." I had very fearlessly compared the young girl to a Greek relief, but when we were out of the hills and were in the meaner villages of the plains I began to feel the truth of that Greek dictum that people can mix too much practice into a theory, especially when it comes to an overwhelming surrender to naturalness. I lost my enthusiasm for my so shortly before uttered panegyric of a world naturally and unconsciously nude. I began to understand a new meaning in the artist's cry of "Give me Naples and her rags!" Especially the rags! Upon some occasions art and sensibility need the rags far more than does morality.

All this argument was with myself as Alfred's dismissal of my tentative first offering on the subject had not been encouraging to further communication. I then proceeded to a further step in my private debate and queried whether in the selection of clothes, to be truly practical, man would not be served better by trusting to comfort rather than to either art or morality. Then I came upon the thought that comfort has no strength to resist convention when they collide. And as convention, with the guile of the serpent, always makes much pretension of riding in the same omnibus with virtue, perhaps after all the true wisdom of life is to stay close to convention. Thus one will be pretty sure to reach Journey's End in good shape. I mentioned my change of heart to Alfred as we were sitting down in the shade of a *ramune* shop, where unabashed nudity had gathered in a circle to regard the foreigners. He did not seem to be moved to interest by my reformation. I heaped a malediction on his head. Surely if I were willing to rearrange my opinions seven times daily at some one stage he might agree.

It was during this rest that I came upon the happiest adventure that the mouth of man may hope to experience in this imperfect world. I had been thirsty from that first day in the East when I had begun breathing in Manchurian dust. In Beijing I had tried to cool my throat by every variety of drink offered through the mingling of Occidental and Oriental civilizations. In Korea, a certain twenty-four hours of wandering alone and lost among the baked and arid mountains had further augmented the parching of my tongue—an increasement which I had believed to be impossible. Along the Tōkaidō we were free to drink as much chemical lemonade as our purse could buy and, despite the warnings of all red-bound guide books, we drank the water. But never, since the beginning of my thirst, had I found a liquid worth one word's praise as a quencher, neither water nor wine, neither *ramune* nor tea. I have irreverently forgotten the name of the village of the discovery.

As we sat resting in the *ramune* shop I looked about and saw some champagne cider bottles of unusually large size. The quantity rather than the flavor of that particular chemical combination was the appeal. I asked for two of the bottles, making the request to a maid who was hoisting a flag over the door. The flag had a single Chinese character printed on it. It was a sign which I later learned to distinguish from incredible distances. After flinging out the flag, she took down two bottles from the shelf but instead of opening them she smiled with a beaming which came from the secure faith that she was bearing good news.

"*Kōri wa ikaga desu ka?*" she asked.

The concluding three words are among the first to be learned from the phrase book and mean "Do you wish?" The word *kōri* I remembered from its having been one of the extras of our first night. It means "ice." We said yes, that we would like ice, but in our ignorance we spoke with no marked ebulliency. She smiled again and sat down, folding her arms in her *kimono* sleeves, an equivalent of that expression of contented virtue shown when our own housewives peacefully wrap their hands in their aprons.

That the flag above the door had some definite meaning for the villagers began to be most evident. The shop was filling. Mob expectancy is contagious and we found ourselves waiting tensely with no clear idea what we were waiting for. The shop was now quite full and all eyes were turned to the street. We heard shouts from the outside that were almost *banzais*, and a coolie came running in. His face was aflame from the happy look of completed service. He was carrying a dripping block of ice in many wrappings of brown hemp cloth. I do not know how far he had come with the ice. Perhaps he had been to some station of the distant railroad. The maid took her hands from her *kimono* sleeves and seized the ice. She pulled off the wrappings. Next she took a saw and cut off an end from the cake. Another maid re-wrapped the precious remainder in the hemp cloth and buried it in a pit dug in the floor. A third maid had been standing by with a board which had a sharp knife edge set into it. The first maid scraped the end of the ice cake over this inverted plane and shavings of sparkling snow fell into her hand. She packed this whiteness into two large, flat, glass dishes. She poured into the snow the effervescing champagne cider and brought us the "adventure."

An adventure is an adventure in proportion to the emotion aroused. For days without end thirst had been sitting astride my tongue. Just as the Old Man of the Sea fastened his thighs around Sindbad's neck and then kicked the poor man's ribs mercilessly with his heels, so had my parasite tickled my throat with its toes. To have unthroned my tormentor at the beginning of its companionship would have been a sensuous satisfaction. To do so after having known the abysses of abject slavery was an ecstasy exceeding the dreams of lovers.

I flushed the ice particles around in my mouth until my eyes rolled in my head. Alfred was alarmed into protests. I had no time to listen. I ordered another bowl of snow and another bottle. It was costing *sen* after *sen* but I knew in my soul that if I had to beg my rice to get to Yokohama and had to sleep under temple steps, even if the price for the snow thus beggared me, the uttermost payment could be in no proportion to the value.

The fertile plain through which the Tōkaidō now wound was crowded with the sight of man. A few houses always clustered wherever a rise in the ground could lift them above the water of the rice fields. The paddy toilers, digging with their hands around the rice roots, worked in long lines, men and women, with their bodies bent flat down from their hips against their legs. If they noticed our passing and looked up, we would say, "It is hot!" and they would say, "It is hot!" Finally an avenue of scrub pines brought shade and I declared for a siesta. Our first attempt gave way before a horde of ants. We tried relaying the top stones of a heap of boulders and then climbed up on that edifice, going to sleep quite contentedly. When I yawned into wakefulness I looked lazily around the landscape wondering where I was. I felt queerly and strangely alone. It was not that the sound of breathing from under Alfred's helmet had ceased. He had not become a deserter, but while we were sleeping every peasant in the fields had disappeared. There can be, then, a degree of heat under which a coolie will not labour, and we had found the day of that heat.

In the next village we discovered our laborers again. They were lying on the floors of their open-sided houses, the elders motionless except for the deep rising and falling of their breasts and an arm lifted now and then in desultory fanning. The children, however, were restless enough to be startled into gazing at the two strangers who were walking the gauntlet of the narrow street.

We had seen an ice flag over a shop at the very entrance to the town but Alfred suggested that there would surely be another shop farther along. I accepted his reasoning but there was not another *kōri* flag to be found anywhere. We had reached the last house. The sign over the shop we had passed was at least a mile back along that burning white gorge. Alfred stopped in at the last house to beg some well water. I looked at the water and thought of the ice.

"If there ever was any ice back there," he said, "it's melted by this time." I was venomous. I left my luggage and started back.

The children, maybe, had been telling their parents of the sight that they had missed, a sight which might never come again. The grinding of my heels this time brought a somewhat larger audience to their elbows. They appeared appreciative of my second appearance. I staggered on and on, mopping my head with a blue and white gift towel. I felt in my limbs the exact strength that would carry me to that *kōri* shop, but to have had to go a foot beyond might well have meant an experience in hallucinations which I had no wish to know.

An old man, who grinned toothlessly, dug down into a sawdust pit and exhumed a fair-sized cake of ice. He moved about his work grotesquely as if he were an animated conceit of carved ivory quickened into life for a moment by the hyper-heat. He at last gave me a bowl of snow with sprinkled sugared water over it. I munched the ice for a full half-hour. As I slowly grew cooler the crowd about me slowly grew larger. They stood silently staring, always staring.

The change for the silver piece which I put down was a heap of coppers. It must have weighed half a pound or more. I might not have been so generous if the wealth had been more portable. As it was, I invited in two or three boys from the circle of the crowd. A carpenter's apprentice had been sitting on the bench beside me. He had paid for one bowl of snow which he had held close to his lips, tossing the sugar powdered ambrosia into his mouth with dexterous flips of a tiny tin spoon. He looked at the ice supply about to disappear into the pit and I invited him to a further participation. He glanced at me intensely for a second as if he wished to solve by that one glance every reason for my existence. Then he turned his attention to his second bowl, which I paid for. His hair was clipped close to his skull. The fresh, youthfully transparent skin of his face was stretched like a sheet of rubber, the tension holding down his nose and allowing his eyes to stare with an openness impossible to optics otherwise socketed.

Just how the round, cannonball head of the Japanese boy evolutes into the featured physiognomy of the Japanese man is puzzling. It must be a sort of bursting. The schoolboy's eyes betray the passing moods of his emotions, but there is always something beyond the mood of the moment in his gazing, an intangible yearning for infinity. It must at times be terrifying for an Anglo-Saxon teacher or missionary to face those eyes. Such a victim may find respite by swearing in the court of all that is practical and material that the mere physical strangeness of the deep staring has bewitched him. He is wise if, by clinging to analysis of the objective world, he can restrain all passion to disturb such mysteries—otherwise he may be led into a voyage such as that of Urashima Tarō to the enchanted island. And then, if ever he seeks to return to his Western identity, he may find that the world which he once knew has died and that he stands neither wedded to the daughter of the Dragon King nor possessing the substance of his former self.

I was thus dreamily communing, studying the face of the carpenter's apprentice. It was he who recalled me from such heat born, mental wanderings by finishing his ice, picking up his *yukata* and throwing it over his shoulder, and walking off with the air of, "Well, you ice dreamer, I have been with you for a moment, but now I have work to do in the world." I followed after him and walked out again into the fiery street.

I can swear that the ice had cooled me back to normal. I felt myself a part of the obvious world. I had banished the disease known as the imagination. I was doing the most practical thing for the moment, going back to my rucksack. But I can also swear that the real world was most unfairly unreal. Great-grandfathers and great-great-grandmothers, who had passed so far along on their journey through life that probably they had given up hope of ever again seeing anything new and worldly strange to interest them, had been carried to the fronts of the houses to behold the outlander. It was as if I had not come to see Japan but Japan had been waiting long and patiently to see me, a parading manikin in a linen suit and yellow boots and a pith helmet. The naked, old, old women, their ribs slowly moving under their dried skin as if breathing and staring were their last hold upon the temporal world, knelt, supported by their children, on the mats. Walking slowly by I felt that I was the sacrificial pageant of the ceremony for their final surrender. There was not a sound from their lips. I began to have a sense of remarkable completeness, that I was a single figure with no possible replica. It was not until I saw Alfred's blue shirt that I was able to snap the thread which was leading me not out of but into the tortuous labyrinth of such speculative folly.

"I was just going back to look for you," he said, "I thought you must have had a sunstroke."

It seemed just then an unnecessary and a too complicated endeavour to explain the minute difference between standing with one's toes on the edge of the calamity which he had feared for me and the actuality of toppling over the precipice. Thus I merely replied that I was feeling all right.

Some tribes of men have in their dogma that the beard must never be trimmed. I am able to imagine that Alfred would carry a sympathetic understanding always with him, no matter among what races he might go adventuring, except into the society of the disbelievers in beard trimming. He demands an extreme exactitude in the trimming of his own beard which proclaims the existence of a certain precise flair of idealism. This flair may be seen manifested in him also in such croppings out as his appreciation for flawless cloisonné. The fact that he had discovered a barber shop and had not made immediate use of his find was overwhelming proof that he had been really solicitous about me. Now that I had returned he made no further delay but sat down in the chair. I stretched out on the matting to wait. The barber's daughter brought cushions and placed them under my head and then knelt at my shoulder to send scurrying breaths of cool air from her fan across my face.

When I awoke Alfred was paying the barber's charge. It amounted, if I remember, to three *sen*, or perhaps three and one-half *sen*. Whatever it was the now properly trimmed *kebukai* foreigner left four *sen* and one-half from his honorable purse, and there was another copper or two as thanks to Momo-*san* for the gentle medicine of her fan.

The barber's clippers, which he had used with such art, had perhaps cost four *yen*. If so, they would—as may be determined by simple division—require at least one hundred similar payments before the return to the barber of their initial cost. There were the razors, and the chair, and the shining cups and bottles, all representing capital outlay. And there must have been rent to pay. There are three demi-gods of the East and only under their reign lies the answer. Great is rice, that it satisfies the hunger. Great is cotton, that it clothes the limbs. Great is art, that it can build the home from the simple bamboo. The barber jingled the four *sen* and a half between his palms, and the jingle was the music that sings of the buying of the rice, the cotton, and the bamboo. There is mystery and magic in economics. And there is, in the submission of man to recognize money as a medium of exchange and in his cooperating to maintain that recognition by law and force, the greatest story in the world.

The barber ceased jingling the coins and dropped them into a drawer. His daughter remained kneeling, her wistful, gentle head bowed low in goodbyes. She had been silent but I imagined that I knew two of her thoughts—no, I should say, two of her moods. One was quite obvious. She had been amused (it was an adventure in its way) to fan to sleep a foreign guest. But the other mood, born of dreaming, was asking where the road led, which those strange visitors were striking out upon, stretching away into the distance as does the march into the beyond of life.

We were talking idly one day with a maid in a certain inn. Her name was Kimi, and she was pretty in the flush of youth, and "very pretty anyhow," as Alfred critically observed. Her feet were quick as sunshine when she ran for our dinner trays, or to bring tea instantly to our room upon our coming in from the street, or to fetch glowing charcoal to our elbow if we should wish to smoke, and her fingers were cunning in all the other little luxuries of service. She was saving money, she said, for the wedding which might be, but as she had neither father nor mother to arrange a marriage she added quite simply that she was only hoping to be married. She desired to wed a merchant, with a shop of his own, having a little room upstairs over the bazaar so that the good wife might be able to run down and attend to customers between domestic duties. She declared an antique shop would be the best, for one can buy nowadays from the wholesalers such wonderful, not-to-be-detected imitations. But her eyes grew sad. It was not within reason to hope that a merchant with such a shop would ever love a dowerless girl, and it was taking so long to save the capital herself. Why, one of the maids of the inn had been there sixteen years! If she had only three hundred *yen* the heaven upon earth might be hers.

I know that Momo-*san*, the daughter of the barber, when she sat wondering what lay beyond the farthest distance she could see along the road, was not imagining a little shop, where between domestic cares she could take time to wait upon customers.

It is for the imagination of dreaming Momo-*san* that the priests light the incense at the sacred altar; it is for practical Kimi-*san* that they read the traditional advice from the theology of moral maxims. The Marys and the Marthas! The cherry blossoms are a bloom of mysterious beauty for the daughter of the barber; they are a symbol of gay festival time for the practical maid of the inn. Will it be the end for the daughter of the barber of Kasada to marry her father's apprentice and to live on in the little shop, dreaming until dreams slumber and are forgotten, knowing only this of the old Tōkaidō that it leads away in a straight line until it is lost in the brilliant blur of the sun on the waters of the rice fields? Or will her imagining heart know adventure in the world beyond the vision of her doorstep? Perhaps the *sen* will come so slowly to the barber's drawer that the wistful daughter will be sold to a *geisha* master, and in filial piety, fulfilling the contract, she may go even to Tokyo where she will be taught to sing and to dance and to laugh gaily. She may find that life is kind. Again, she may be sold to another life— under the juggernaut of poverty—and in the Nightless City knowledge will come to dwell in the empty place where wistfulness was.

We walked away from Kasada along the unchanging road. One blade of rice was like another, one step was like another, finally one thought became like another. Nagoya was many miles ahead. Alfred, the tramper, is of the faith which holds that to give in to a stretch of road just because it is dull is to surrender for no reason at all. That is good doctrine. I have something of it, but my hold upon the faith is admixed with a Catholicism which does not preclude the restful and inward harmony of maintaining speaking acquaintance with several conflicting beliefs. On the other hand Alfred will, simply and unostentatiously, subordinate his preferences, but the surrender is so generous that that virtue is usually a protection in itself against applied selfishness. To escape any disagreeable feeling of shame I thought it might be that Alfred could be induced to make the suggestion himself that we take some more rapid means of transportation. We were in the land of *jūjūtsu*. The fundamental idea of this system is that you politely assist your opponent to throw himself. I began by alluding to the thrills and possibilities of the antique shops of Nagoya. If we should continue walking we could not reach there until late at night, and if we should find Hori Kenjirō waiting for us and prepared to be off early the next morning, when would there be time for exploring? I then ventured casually that the railroad would take us to Nagoya in a couple of hours. Imagination began to work as my ally. Alfred at last queried directly whether I would be willing to give up walking in the country for exploration in the city. I yielded. Thus, when the arrogant Tōkaidō of steel crossed our road, as the map had told me it soon would, two foreigners with rucksacks found places amid teapots and babies, bundles and ever fanning elders, and soon they saw the tall smokestacks of modern Nagoya.

Our kit of clean linen and clean suits had been forwarded from Kyoto in care of the foreign hotel. Perhaps we each had had the idea when the bag was packed that we would be exceedingly content to catch up with it again, not alone for the contents but in anticipation that the finding would mean that we would be again surrounded by the comfort of Western standards exotically flourishing. Alas for the stability of our tenet! We were aware that our capitulation to the simplicity of the native inns sprang partly from the glamour of the new, but the conquest had come from realization and not mere anticipation. Dilettantes we were, truly, and as such we acknowledged ourselves, but we should be credited that we escaped the eczema of reformers. We had no obsession to hasten back to our own land to argue the multitudes out of the custom of wearing shoes in the house or sitting on chairs instead of floors. Nevertheless when we walked into the door of the hotel and up the stairs every tread of our heavy, dusty boots struck at our sensibility of a better fitness and order.

We walked along the upstairs hall and passed a room with wide open double doors. There was Hori Kenjirō waiting for us—that is, a semblance of Hori-*san* was there, his material body. When a Japanese sleeps his absorption by his dream hours is so complete that one is tempted to believe that his so-called waking hours (no matter how manifested in energy) may be only a hazy interim between periods of a much more important psychic existence. We walked into the room and sat down and talked things over and waited for the opening of Kenjirō's eyelids, but they moved not. Alfred at last departed to seek treasure trove in the antique shops and I decided for the laziness of a bath.

I asked for a hot bath. The bath boy's uniform was starched and new, and he was starched and new in his position as drawer of water. He was very proud of such responsibility and was very earnest and very smiling. In some other occupation he had picked up a little English. He promised to hurry. Minutes went by. Above the sound of the running of the water I could hear a mysterious pounding and scraping. This combination of noises continued with no regard for passing time. Now and again I pounded on the door in Occidental impatience. "Very quick! Very quick!" would come his answer. When the bolt did snap back I could see from his perspiring face that he must have been hurrying after some fashion of his own. He bowed and pointed to the tub. I put in one foot—and out it came. The water might have come from a glacier.

"I asked for a hot bath—*o-yu, furo*," I shouted.

There was no retreat of the smiles. They even grew.

"Japanese man, he take hot bath. Foreign man, he take cold bath."

I now understood the scraping and pounding. The hot days had attacked the water tanks of the hotel until the faucets marked "Cold" were running warm. The bath boy had been laboriously stirring around a cake of ice in the tub. Blandly came the repetition, "Foreign man, he take cold bath."

For the sake of sweet courtesy and kindly appreciation I should have sat down in that water, but I did not. I pulled out the stopper and drew a hot tub. When the boy realized this sacrilege against the custom of the foreign man, he veritably trembled from the violence of the restraint which he had to put upon himself, but his idea of courtesy was so far superior to mine that he retreated. I bolted the door against him.

Alfred returned from his field with enraptured accounts. There is some sort of affinity between him and a bit of treasure. He is the hazel wand and the antique is the hidden water, but as a human divining rod he does not merely bend to magnetism, he leaps. My first initiation to that knowledge had been so sufficiently striking that no new evidences ever surprised me. That initiation had come when we were riding one Sunday morning on the top of a tram in the cathedral city of Bath. We were in the midst of a discussion. Half way through a sentence he suddenly lifted himself over the rail and disappeared down the side of the car. When I could finally alight more conventionally I ran back to find him with his nose against a dull and uninviting window. From the top of the tram he had seen within the shadows a chair. There was no arousing the antique shop on Sunday and thus he left a note of inquiry under the door and eventually that particular treasure, wrapped in burlap, made its long journey to America.

He began discussing the treasures of Nagoya when in walked Kenjirō.

"I don't see how you got by my door," he said.

"Weren't you asleep?" I asked.

"Oh, just dozing," he explained.

The Ancient Nakasendō

We had an hour to kill before dinner and we were irritably moody against the foreign windows which gave us no breeze. "It's housely hot," said Alfred, and he sighed pathetically for the cool mats of an inn floor where there would be a pot of freshly brewed tea at his elbow and a green garden to look out upon. I was studying a map of Japan, tracing out its rivers and mountains.

I have an inordinate passion for maps. Surely Stevenson had some such passion. I venture that he first thought of the pirate's chart of "Treasure Island" and after that first imagination the story simply wrote itself. Particularly does passion find satisfaction in one of the old Elizabethan maps, printed in full, rich colors, the margins portraying the waves of the sea with dolphins diving, and with barques straining under bellied sails. Some are headed for the Spanish Main, and others are striking out for the regions marked "Unknown." Those old Elizabethan maps could have been drawn only in the days of hurly-burly England when the deep-chested seamen under Raleigh and Drake sang savage sea songs in the taverns and the tingling life in a man's veins was worth its weight in adventure. No wonder that today, with our pale, lithographed maps telling us the exact number of nautical miles to the farthest coral island we have become analytic and scientific. As Okakura said, "We are modern, which means that we are old." Nevertheless, a pale, errorless, unemotional map is better than no map at all.

The particular map of Japan which I was studying had had a few mysteries added in the printing which were not to be blamed upon the geographer. The different colors had been laid on by the printer with marked independence of registration. It was difficult to trace even the old Tōkaidō, but imagination from practical experience told me that when it followed the coast it led through miles and miles of rice fields. Farther up on the map, in the mountain ranges above Nagoya, I saw a blurred word and turning the sheet on end I read "Nakasendō."

The word brought a remembrance. I began trying to piece together what that memory was. At last I assembled a forgotten picture of a Japanese whom I had once met on a train. In the beginning I had thought him a modern of the moderns until he told me of his sacred pilgrimages. It was my surprise, I suppose, in his tale of his tramping, staff in hand, with the peasants that had made me so distinctly remember his earnestness as he mouthed the full word "Nakasendō." I rolled over on the bed with my finger on the map and asked Kenjirō if he had ever heard of the Nakasendō.

Kenjirō looked up in surprise as if I had rudely mentioned some holy name. "All day," he said, "I have been thinking of the Nakasendō." Then he told us how the Nakasendō road enters the mountains through the valley of the beautiful Kiso River and, following the ranges first to the north and then to the east, takes its way to Tokyo. In the era before railroads it was a great arterial thoroughfare and in those feudal days the *daimyō* of the north and their retainers journeyed the Nakasendō route with as much pomp as did their southern rivals along the Tōkaidō. Nevertheless the Nakasendō now exists in history as the less famous thoroughfare of the two. Kenjirō suggested that the dimming of its fame may have come because its ancient followers had cherished its beauty with such intensity that they did not allow their artists to paint it nor their poets to sing of it to the world, in the belief, perhaps, that all objective praise could be but supererogation.

I had most of this imagining from Kenjirō's understatements rather than from anything definite that he said. He is of the *samurai* and his ancestors learned the art of conversation in a court circle devoted to the graces. The incompleted phrase of the East so subtly makes one an accessory in the creation of the idea involved that we, of the West, who live in a world of overstatement, find ourselves disarmed to deny. One cannot discount words that have never been uttered.

I added to Kenjirō's words some definite phrases from my own imagination. These were to influence Alfred if possible. I knew that it had been his long held dream to walk the Tōkaidō from end to end, but I had not realized until I saw his dismay at my suggestion of a change how ardent his dream had been. I had recklessly prophesied the mountains of the Nakasendō to be the abode of spring among other praises. It could not be denied that whatever the Tōkaidō was or was not, the rice fields that had to be crossed would not be springlike.

We slept over such argument as we had had. The next day burst in the glory of a burning sun, which was rather an argument on the side of the mountain faction. The breakfast butter melted before our eyes. Alfred finished his marmalade and pushed back his chair, and then casually capitulated. "Well," he said, "if we are going to the mountains, what are we waiting for?" What indeed? I ran upstairs to our room and pulled off my hotel-civilization clothes and stuffed them into the bag and labelled it for Yokohama. There was to be no more formal emerging into the *seiyō-jin*'s world for us until we should reach that port of compulsion. Alfred was less exuberant in his packing but he cheerfully whistled some air—which was indeed forgiving—and as usual was ready before I was.

Kenjirō's travelling kit had evidently bothered him not at all. A half-dozen collars, two or three books, one or two supplementary garments, and a straw hat were tied up in a blue and orange handkerchief and this *furoshiki* was tied to the handlebars of a bicycle. Until we met the bicycle we had talked of the problems and plans of the three of us, but from the instant of production there was no gainsaying that there were four of us. Further, the really colorful and unique personality among the four partners of the vagabondage was that diabolical, mechanical contraption.

In making that machine, the manufacturer, without possibility of dispute, had achieved the supremacy of turning out the most consistently jerry-built affair since the beginning of time. He merits first immortality both in any memorialization by the shades of jerry-builders who have gone before and in the future from the tribe as it expands and multiplies upon the earth. The loose, and often parting, chain hung from sprocket wheels that marvellously revolved at nearly right angles to each other. When Kenjirō mounted into the saddle the wheels fearsomely bent under his weight until their circumferences advanced along the road in ellipses strange and unknown to the plotting of calculus. The rims scraped the mudguards in continuous rattle as if there were not enough other grinding sounds of despair coming from every gear and bearing. In some way those abnormalities worked together, acting in compensation. Any one of the single errors without such correspondingly outrageous offset would have been prohibitive to locomotion.

The indomitable spirit of the machine to keep going should perhaps be praised, but its general character was steeped in malevolency against all human kind. It hated Kenjirō no less violently than it did us or strangers. It hated and was hated and continued to leave a trail of hatred in its path until a certain memorable day when we came to a mountain climb. While we were discussing what best could be done for its transport the proud spirit overheard that it would have to submit to being tied upon a coolie's back. It rebelled into heroic suicide at that prospect. It committed *harakiri*. The entire mechanism collapsed suddenly into an almost unrecognizable wreck.

"When the flower fades," says Okakura Kakuzo, "the master tenderly consigns it to the river or carefully buries it in the ground. Monuments are even sometimes erected to their memory." Kenjirō gave a piece of money to the coolie for a reverent burial of the demon wheel.

Our breakfast had really been luncheon and after our energy of packing and getting started we so indulged our time in the shops on the way out of the city that we finally decided that if we were to get into the mountains before night we should have to take the train over the paddy fields. The bicycle, the rucksacks, and the blue and orange handkerchief, together with the owners, were crowded into an accommodation train. The small engine puffed with the temperament of a nervous pomeranian, throwing a volcanic spume into the air which condensed into a fine diamond ash to come back to earth and to stream into the windows and then to drift, eddy, and scurry about the seats and floor.

An accommodation train has the verve of life which the conventions of a through express stifle. But whether it be a New England local with bird cages, or the Italian *misti* with priests and snuff boxes, nursing madonnas, garlic sandwiches, and chianti bottles, or the stifling wooden boxes of Northern India crowded with Afridi and Babus, no train in all the world is as domestic as the Japanese *kisha*. Friends and the friends of friends come to rejoice in the dramatic formalities of farewell. If perchance any individual on the platform is neither the friend nor the friend of a friend of some departing one he takes an altruistic pleasure in smiling upon the opportunities of others.

We bought our pots of tea with tiny earthenware cups attached and put them on the floor as did everyone else. We also bought our *bentō* boxes, of rice, raw fish, pickles, seaweed, and bamboo shoots, from the criers of "*Bentō! Bentō!! Bentō!!!* The train started. No one was bored, the children were not restless, and we of our carriage stayed awake or went to sleep in every posture possible to the flexibility of human limbs matched against the rigidity of wooden seats. The babies came along and became acquainted and we sent them back to their parents carrying gifts of cigarettes.

Curled up on the seat across from ours, with her head resting on her luggage, was a girl about twenty years of age. She was a Eurasian and was beautiful rather than pretty. Now and again her graceful arm raised her fan but otherwise she did not move. Her dark eyes returned no curious glances. Her mood of mind and soul seemed as frozen and hard as the blue ice of a mountain glacier. It was a passionate negativity, her defense against the instinct of society, which eternally wages war upon the hybrid. It is instinctive, this struggle of the race mass mind against the disintegration of its integrity. She had learned the meaning of glances. The Eurasian must expiate a guiltless guilt. She did not ask for quarter in the battle. Far behind that cold, defensive gaze was the strength of two proud races. Character makes fate, said the Greeks. Inevitability may make tragedy. We were to pick up the threads of old tales of love and tragedy along the valley of the Kiso River, but in the life of that strange, fearless, beautiful Eurasian girl was the web and woof of a yet uncompleted story. When we at last passed our bundles out of the window at Agematsu she had not stirred.

We had been carried out of the plains and night was coming down. Kenjirō voiced an inquiry about our landing spot. It was indeed high time to be located some place for dinner and the night. Our indifference to particularization about our landing had begun to harass him. In Kobe and Nagoya when our surpassing indefiniteness had come out he had nodded and said, "yes," evidently putting his faith in the belief that there would surely be an eventual limit to such casualness. I was slow to realize his worry but when I did some primitive idea of justice told me that his breaking into the inefficiency of our methods ought to be more gentle and gradual. I whispered this intuition to Alfred and thus, when the train halted at the next platform, out went our luggage and we were left standing to watch the fiery cloud of cinders disappear into the blue-grey mist.

It had grown cold. The rain was curiously like snow, drifting through the air, seemingly without weight. There was the beginning of a path up a slippery clay hill, the upper reaches of which were lost in fog and darkness. Even the short distances of vision, which until then had endured, succumbed before we had scrambled up the hill. We made a careful reconnaissance with hands and feet and found that the mountain path at the top branched in several directions. The town might lie in any direction. For more meditative cogitation Kenjirō carefully lowered the bicycle to its side but unfortunately there was no ground beneath and off it slid. We heard it painfully scraping down the rocks. In Alpine fashion we had to go after it. We crawled back again to stand in a circle on the road, drenched and mud covered.

Dinner, bed, and bath might be within a hundred yards but to take the wrong path might mean to wander until sunrise. At least so we thought. Such a variety of adventure is much more interesting in retrospect than prospect. However, it was worse to stand still. We started on an exploration, craftily putting the bicycle next to the precipice. On peaceful days the gears often meshed in moderate quietness but at any time when its companions failed in omnipotent judgment they would grind out a wailing reiteration of: "I told you so. I told you so." We were shuffling along to the measure of that lamentation when suddenly there was a sparkle of light ahead. It was from a lantern. The bearer was a peasant bundled up in a rush grass cape. He lifted the light into our faces and then gave a single sharp cry of fear. Next he shut his eyes tightly and was speechless.

A well-balanced consideration for the rights of one's brothers is intended for normal times. Now that a guide had offered himself to us out of the darkness we purposed to keep him, although for a few minutes he seemed a rather useless discovery. Kenjirō managed at length to pry the man's eyes open with wet fingers and, then with fair words sought to persuade him that if we were not ghosts we obviously needed his help, but that if we were, then any sense left in him should tell him that it would be far better to listen to our request to guide us to an inn and to leave us there than to risk our trailing him to his own home. He grasped Kenjirō's point. We followed after our guide and, as we had suspected, the distance to the village was only a few steps. At the threshold of the inn our guide bolted. If he had been cherishing a grudge he should have waited to see our reception. It was not pleasing to us.

Kenjirō advanced into the courtyard to engage in Homeric debate. The fog sweeping in struggled with the lights of the lanterns and candles. The picture was a theatrical composition. There were the three rain-soaked, laden intruders facing the maid-servants. The maids' *kimono* sleeves were pinned back to their shoulders and their skirts were gathered up through their girdles. Their faces and limbs gleamed in the coppery light. The door to the steaming kitchen opened on to the courtyard and within its shadows the pots and kettles hanging on the walls caught the glowing flame of the charcoal. I suppose there was not a more honest inn in all the land but the wild, picaresque picture suggested an imagining by Don Quixote painted by Rembrandt or Hogarth or Goya. It was a point of immediate reality, however, which concerned us, and that point was that we were so far in the inn but no farther, and no farther did we get.

They gave a reason. They said that the inn was full. It seemed so ridiculous to have had such trouble in finding an inn and then to lose it that Alfred and I began laughing. We laughed inordinately, but our barbarous merriment brought our listeners no nearer to changing their conviction that the inn was full. There was another inn farther down the street, they said, and we borrowed a lantern and a coolie from them and started. The coolie ran ahead and when we arrived at the second inn the mistress and all her maid-servants were at the door. From the length of Kenjirō's argument I became suspicious that we again were not considered desirable, but after a time he turned and said: "It's all right."

As soon as we were in our room, hurriedly getting ready for the bath, I tried to find out from Kenjirō what the long debate was about, but English is evidently much more laconic than Japanese. He summed it all up by saying that they feared the inn was unworthy of foreigners. Admirable *bushidō*! What inn in the wide world could have been worthy of such bedraggled wanderers? However, once we were allowed within the walls and recognized as guests the spirit of hospitality welled solicitously.

Listen, O dogmatists! The joy of the finding is not always less than the joy of the pursuit. If there are doubters let them seek the Nakasendō trail and find the second inn of Agematsu, there to learn that no dinner that they have ever imagined can equal the realization they will discover inside the lacquer bowls and porcelain dishes which will be brought to them.

The maid who had been assigned to administer to our comfort accepted her duty as a trust. She was unbelievably short, but was very sturdy. Her broad face and the strength of her round, unshaped limbs proclaimed the hardy bloom of the peasantry. The physical, mental, and emotional unity which comes as the heritage of such unmixed rustic blood is in itself a pre-possessing charm. Our daughter of Mother Earth was as maternal as she was diminutive. She might think of a thousand services, her bare feet might start of an instant across the mats to respond to any requests, but never did she surrender one iota of her instinctive belief that we, merely being men, were only luxurious accessories for the world to possess. She was so pri-mordially feminine that she inspired a terrifying thought of the possibility of society being sometime modelled after the queendom of the bees.

She had never seen a foreigner but she had heard much gossip of our strange customs. Her inquiring mind was intent upon verifying this gossip as far as possible. She was also very curious about our possessions. She taught us how to hold our chopsticks and how to drink our soup. She told us that we drank too silently. A little more noise from our lips, she said, would show that we were appreciating the flavor. She did acknowledge in us some aptitude to learn, implying that if a more advanced state of culture had existed in the feminine family group of our homes over the seas we might have been mothered into some respectability. So saying, she arose sturdily to her full height and bore away the dinner tables. Then she returned to make the beds, struggling with the mattresses as might an ant dragging oak leaves.

When the beds were finally laid she brought a fresh brewing of tea and replenished the charcoal in the *hibachi*. She lighted our after-dinner cigarettes for us by pressing them against the embers. She sat waiting until we had dropped the last stub into the ashes. Then guardian midget rolled back the quilts, ordered us to bed, tucked us in carefully, giving to each impartially a good-night pat. Her day's work finished, assuredly her efforts entitled her to a quiet enjoyment of one of the cigarettes! She sat down on the foot of my bed and deeply drawing in the smoke, blew it into the air with a sigh of contentment.

"I have been told," she said, "that foreigners marry for love. Can that be true?" We assured her that that custom existed.

"Um-m-m," she pondered. Our examination was evidently of import. She took another step in questioning.

"But if you married for love how can you be happy to travel so far away from your wives?"

She gasped at our claim of non-possession.

We made a second insistence regarding our unsocial state. She did not put aside her good nature but she berated us roundly for our unkindness, our lack of taste, in thinking that we could joke in such a way just because she was a peasant girl in a country inn, but when we further insisted upon repeating our tale she was really hurt. There is a time, she said, for joking to come to an end. If it were always thus our custom to insist upon a joke long after it had been laughed at and appreciated, then she did not believe that she had excessive pity for our wives and children in their being left behind while we wandered.

She then dismissed us from her questioning and appealed exclusively to Kenjirō. She could understand that if we had been forced to marry by parental social regulation and had been united to wives whom we did not and could not love, perhaps it would be quite within reason that we should wish to have vacations in singleness, but to have had the privilege of marrying for love and then to be wandering alone—oh, it was un-understandable.

"Well," said Kenjirō mysteriously, "I think that what they have said is the truth but it may not be all the truth. In their country certain desperately wicked criminals are not allowed the privilege of marrying."

There is a glamour which hangs over the notoriously wicked. The maid's glances were now modified by appropriate awe into distinct respect. She got up, and endeavoring for dignity built a tower out of the scattered cushions. She climbed upon this shaky height and turned out the light. Then she hurried away to the backstairs regions with her tale.

In the morning it was raining. When we got up we could hear no sounds below and when we went to the bath there were no maids to fill the brass basins. Kenjirō wandered off to the kitchen to find hot water and we did not see him again until after our maid, very heavy-eyed, had brought the breakfast tables to our room. He came as the bearer of two items of information which he had gleaned from the mistress. The first was that there had been a council sitting on our morals, presided over by our maid, which had lasted through the hours of the night. The second item was the truthful reason why we had been turned away from the first inn and the confirmation of our suspicions that we had gained admittance where we were only by an extremely narrow margin.

Once upon a time two foreigners had passed through Agematsu and had been received as guests in one of the inns. That advent had been so many years before that a new generation of mistresses and maids had succeeded the victims of the marvellous invasion, but the legend of that night of terror had been handed down undimmed. "And what do you think was their unspeakable atrocity?" Kenjirō asked dramatically. "*They made snowballs from the rice of the rice box at dinner and threw them at each other and at the maids!*"

From time to time, through the mountains, we heard again the legend of those two remarkable *seiyō-jin*. We grew to have an admiration for knaves so lusty in their revels that they could leave behind such a never fading flower of memory. They must have gone forth to their travels minutely familiar with the code of Japanese etiquette, so thoroughly were they skilled in fracturing it. A riot might have been forgiven, and forgotten, but not the throwing of rice on the floor. The one constant forbidding under which a child is brought up finally leaves no process of thought in the brain that anyone could ever intentionally offend against the cleanness of the matting. It is less a *gaucherie* to set fire to a friend's house and burn it to the ground than to spill a bowl of soup.

We waited for the rain to clear away, but as it did not we borrowed huge paper umbrellas and wandered off down the valley. We were in the midst of a silk spinning district and in almost every doorway sat some woman of the household busily capturing the silken threads from the cocoons. We asked permission to rest in the door of a carpenter's shop which overhung the rocky Kiso River and was shaded by the tops of great pines which grew from the sides of the valley bed. The carpenter brought us tea and stopped for a moment to point the view through the trees which had been the companion of his life.

Sometimes poverty seems to be an absolute and unarguable condition. At other times one's ideas as to the what and when of poverty are so shifting as merely to be interrogations. There was the poverty in that valley of the struggle for some slight margin above dire want: the silk workers were speeding their machines for their pittance, the carpenter was busy through every hour of daylight. Economics and efficiency are everyday words but what is their ultimate meaning not in dollars but in life? What are the real wishes of the leaders in Tokyo, the statesmen who are planning policies and at the same time must strive to please the great banking houses of the world?—do they look forward to the time when factories will fill the land and the spinners will not be sitting in their own doorways but the children of today's workers will be standing in long rows before machines? "We are taught," explained a Japanese, "to pay our heavy taxes cheerfully so that the empire may expand and develop. Wealth will be thus created and then taxes can be reduced."

Kenjirō had remembrance of a traveller's tale which he had heard long before of an ancient tea-house along the Kiso River famous both for its noodle soup and its view of the spot locally believed to have been the awakening place of Urashima when he returned from the Island of the Dragon King. Considering that the story explicitly states that Urashima awoke on the seashore, the faith of the inland believers is really more marvellously imaginative than the story itself. The trudging coolies whom we stopped had never heard of the tea-house. Therefore we knocked at the first gate we came to in the bamboo wall along the road to find that our footsteps had magically led us to the famed spot itself. We left our muddy boots at the door and a maid showed us the way to the balcony of the room of honor from which we could see the tumbling river. The view is called "The Awakening." An islet emerges from the foam of the waters and its rocks have been made to serve as a miniature temple garden. There is another view farther down the bank, from which the dwarfed pines and stone lanterns of the island may be seen to better advantage. Cicerones lie in wait there for the sightseer. In delightful contrast to the urgings generally experienced from the tribe, these guides were quite shy in the presence of foreigners.

The daughter of the house, in a *kimono* of silk and brocade, herself brought the tray of tea and *sake* and a pyramid dish of noodles. The porcelain was old and of tempting beauty. The tea was fragrant. Kenjirō insisted that we should extemporize poetry to express our appreciation of the beauty of the Kiso River, but Alfred and I were rather self-conscious in our rhymes. We had been nurtured in a land of specialization where poetry is entrusted to professionals. The sun came out. We paid our reckoning, folded up our paper umbrellas, and walked back to our inn for a long night's sleep.

The Bottle Inn

In the morning Kenjirō discovered that his military survey map somehow had been mistaken for a sheet of wrapping paper the day before. The torn-off section had served to carry rice cakes in my pocket. The tearing had strangely traversed mountains, valleys, and rivers along almost the line we intended to follow. As Kenjirō was still unemancipated from the idea that not to know where one is is to be lost, he was rather in a maze for the next few days, as we continually wandered off the edge of the map into unknown regions. He must have marvelled at times over the kindness of the Providence that had guided our steps from Kyoto to Nagoya.

The valley of the Kiso River earnestly seeks to attest the theory that the inhabitants of localities with a similar climate and topography tend to have similar ideas, especially in working out ways of doing the same thing. The wide sweeping view with the snow-topped mountains on the horizon might have been Switzerland, and for a more decisive deceiving of the eye into thinking so the cottages of the peasants had the overhanging roof of the Swiss chalet with the same pitch and the same arrangement of rows of boulders on them. It is a province, also, of trousered women.

We came upon a wistful-eyed, pink-cheeked, timid fairy of the mountains. She was carrying on her back a huge, barrel-shaped basket and she bent forward as she slowly walked along, her eyes fixed on a handful of wild flowers in her fingers. Even our modest knowledge of the folklore of the land told us that she must be a princess who had been captured by ugly trolls. They had set her to impossible labour as their revenge against her beauty. A young man whose niche in the world was beyond our determining—although we thought he might be a student on a vacation walking trip—had caught up with us a half-hour before and had been measuring his step with ours. When he discovered that I wished to take a picture of the princess he assisted with such effective blandishment of speech that she halted for an instant. When I asked that I might also photograph him, he laughed and vaulted up among the rocks and disappeared.

A little farther along we met the six sisters of the princess. They were carrying burdens equally as large and heavy as had she, but they were not so pretty nor so wistful, albeit they were just as timid. We never could find any key to the mystery why our appearance along the highway would sometimes be as startling as if we were ghostly apparitions, and at other times it would merely bring about a casual interest and staring, if it brought any interest at all. Upon this occasion it was a panic. The six maidens beheld us, they shrieked in unison, and they jumped from the road, trying to hide behind rocks and trees. Their lithe limbs might have carried them like fawns, if their shoulders had been freed from the huge baskets, but, as it was, their flight was more like that of some new and enormous variety of the beetle tribe, evoluted so far as to wear cotton clothes and to have pretty human heads turbaned under blue and white handkerchiefs. As a son of Daguerre, I should have tarried for an instant to photograph their amazing struggle, but an upsetting obsession of chivalry hurried us on. By the time we turned to look back they had scrambled to the road, all six princesses accounted for. They, too, turned to look at us and from the safety of distance began to laugh. The comedy might thus have ended if it had not been that at that instant Kenjirō rounded the bend of the road with his thumb pressed vigorously against the strident bicycle bell. The beetles (or, better to say, the wingless butterflies) again took flight. We awaited their second reappearance. This time they did not venture laughter until they reached the curve and made sure of no further dismay.

Kenjirō dismounted and pushed the bicycle along and we entered into one of our unending discussions. A subject sometimes in debate was Alfred's and my intense interest—our curiosity—in the conversations that Kenjirō had with passersby along the road or in the shops. Sometimes, when we

had made some simple inquiry in a shop, Kenjirō would ask a long question;
the shopkeeper would answer; Kenjirō would enter a counter dissertation;
the shopkeeper would make his reply to that; Kenjirō would reply; the
shopkeeper would reply; Kenjirō would reply; and then it might be that
the shopkeeper would have the conclusion. Kenjirō might then turn to us
with: "He says 'no.'"

In the port city shops where English is spoken, if there is but one clerk
he will answer your questions immediately. If there are two, every question
is thoroughly discussed in Japanese before answering, and if there be three,
four, or five clerks, the debate goes on to extraordinary length. Again and
again we asked Kenjirō for a complete translation but it must have been
that he believed within himself that he had asked the question in the simplest
terms, for we seldom got a verbatim translation.

We were in the midst of some such discussion when we looked up to see
an old man standing before us, leaning on a long staff. His white beard fell
benignly and his steady eyes carried a message of goodwill. He returned
our greetings by a dignified inclination of his head. We were at the peak of
the road and, as often may be found at such points, there was a small rest
tea-house for travellers. We asked the old man if he would sit down with
us and share a pot of tea.

The iron pot, filled with mountain spring water, steamed hospitably on
the *hibachi* and the fragrance of the tea was a friendly invitation to relax.
Our guest stood his long staff in the corner, sat down on a cushion, and
drew his feet from his dusty sandals. After the true manner of happily met
travellers he was easily persuaded to tell us the tale of his wanderings. The
translation is somewhat rhetorical but, as Kenjirō explained, the tale was
told in the language of etiquette.

"I was born," he said, "in the forty-first year of the rule of the *Shōgun*
Ienari. I was young and am now old. My eighty and seven summers have
seen the downfall of the once mighty before the rising to full glory of the
Meiji, and now, from the Palace of Edo, shine upon us the divine rays of
the Way of Heaven. Great is the Mercy of Enlightenment. The Eternal Glory
is the Way.

"As a child I knew these mountains which you see. The provinces of our
land were then fortified by many castles and these roads were traversed by

armed men. The castles have been razed to the ground but the temples of
the gods still stand. The two-sworded warriors have gone but I, a humble
pilgrim, walk the roads they once knew. The white clouds rest in the blue
sky above Mount Fuji, or Fuji-*san*, as when I looked upon them as a child.
The clouds will rest above Fuji-*san* when these eyes shall see them not.

"In the fourteenth year of my youth I took the vow that my life should
be lived in honoring the holy images of Buddha, each and all as my steps
might find them, from the shrines erected by the peasants to the bronze
statues of the great temples. I took the very staff which you see and the
clothes that were upon my back and bade my family goodbye. Through the
kindness in the hearts of men, the lowly and the mighty, the gods have
provided me with food and rest. I have travelled without illness and my
spirit has known the joy of the Way."

In those years that his bowl had not gone empty of rice, never, it may be
believed, did anyone give to him as a beggar asking. Japan is of the East,
possessing the intuition that the spiritual is a mystic interflow.

His eyes were young; they were not clouded in contemplation of the
abstract. They sparkled from a delight in life. It had not been demanded of
him that his vicarious pilgrimage should be one of tragic sacrifice. He had
given and he had received. While his theoretical faith might be that life is
an illusion and only the Way is eternal, nevertheless he was born to love
his fellowmen and he could not escape from the practical faith that was in
him that this temporal life must be of some use and of some meaning. I
remembered in strange comparison a sturdy British unemployed whom I
had once come upon. He was lying under a hedge in Monmouthshire. He
borrowed a pipeful of tobacco and then turned over onto his back to gaze
into the blue sky. After a time he said: "Activity is a fever. Therefore it is
a disease. Laziness is a promise. Rest and forgetfulness are divine." He did
not make the effort to add a goodbye when I left him.

A path of our pilgrim led over the road which we had just travelled. We
parted, bowing many times. Kenjirō unfolded his ravaged map and found
a village named Narii a few miles farther along. The railroad down in the
valley according to the map went somewhere near Narii. Kenjirō's nerves
had been rasped by the temperamental vagaries of the bicycle on the steep
slopes and he decided to await a train, promising to meet us.

After a time our path dropped down to the bed of the river. Across a bridge the road forked, one branch continuing along the valley and the other winding off into the hills. The hill trail, particularly as it led into the unknown regions off Kenjirō's map, tempted, and we shouted down an inquiry to some children playing in the water. They were successfully attempting to get as wet as possible while remaining as dirty as possible. There is a mystery which overhangs grimy Japanese children. When the little noses present a constant temptation to the *seiyō-jin* handkerchief that in itself is a caste sign that you will find the faces of their fathers and mothers unhappy, dull, and lustreless. When the children are brightly scoured and polished there is a general appearance of happiness and contentment in the community. It is not the simple equation that poverty equals dirt. One village is scrubbed and the next one is not—otherwise neither seems richer nor poorer except in happy looks.

When we called to the children in the Kiso River they splashed out of the water like wild animals and scattered in all directions, but as two naked infants too small to run had been left on the shore, first the girls and then the boys began to edge back. They remained to stare. We pointed up the mountain path and asked if it led to Narii. Their gestures evinced a fierce encouragement to essay the ridges as if they had the contempt of the untamed for anything as conventional as a broad valley road. As a matter of fact they were undoubtedly saying that the valley road did not lead to Narii. We discovered this later when we could look down from the heights. Kenjirō's railroad tunnelled the hills.

According to local belief our path carried us over the "backbone" of the empire, and this crossing spot is considered sacred ground. Accordingly we should have paid special homage to the local deity whose shrine we passed, but as we were foreigners and in ignorance, the god perhaps forgave us. Furthermore, we unknowingly passed a particularly renowned view of very holy Mount Ontake. We probably did see the mountain, but being uninformed, as I said, of this special view, we did not hold ourselves in proper restraint until reaching the exact spot for appreciation. Instead we luxuriously and squanderously revelled in all four directions of the compass. It is always thus with the ignorant. Their indiscriminate enthusiasm is more irritating to the intellectuals than no appreciation at all. I was later most depressingly snubbed for having missed the sacred view by a scholar of things Japanese. He knew it from prints and sacred writings. He said that he himself would have journeyed to see the reality if it had not been for the probable annoyance of having to come in contact with so many natives on the journey. He appeared to be impatient that the British Museum does not commandeer all views, temples, and abiding places of art around the world and establish turnstiles which will keep the natives out and let the scholars in. When he actually grasped that our only reason for having arrived at that particular spot at all was that we had taken a turning to the right instead of to the left, he declared that our ideas of travelling evidence the same intelligence as might the tripping of tumbling beans and that our very presence at sacred places was a sacrilege.

We turned a corner that hung sharply over the precipice. Around the bend the shelf spread out into a miniature meadow. A peasant was lying on the grass and his straw-bonneted ox was leisurely nibbling. We sat down beside him and Alfred began searching in his rucksack for a remaining cake of chocolate. During this hunt the peasant kept his eyes carefully and earnestly averted. I made the remark to him that the view was *kirei* and he replied by a nervous *hai*. Alfred found the chocolate and broke it into three parts. He handed one of the squares to the peasant. The fingers that reached out for it were trembling.

The man had imaginative eyes. It was plain to see that he was suffering from some lively remembrance of a mountain folklore demon story. He knew that we were foxes or badgers who had assumed human form, and that we had come to him with no good intentions. He suspected a subtle poison. But he had courage from one thought. It is the common knowledge of the countryside that while the demands of demon badgers may not be directly refused, their evil intent may often be thwarted by the crafty intelligence of man. The immediate problem was how to avoid the appearance of refusing to eat the mysterious cake which was now getting soft and moist in his hand. Suddenly he popped the chocolate into his mouth, tin foil and all. Then he pushed back the square into his hand almost in the same movement. I pretended not to be watching. He dropped his hand with elaborate carelessness into the thickness of the grass. I felt a sense of dramatic relievement myself.

During those minutes the ox had been no such respecter of enchantment as had his master. Instead, he had stood sniffing at our boots and pulling up bits of grass round and about our ankles, all the time rolling a pair of red, angry eyes. Asiatic beasts of burden find something antagonistic to their complaisance in the odors of the Caucasian and this individual ox was progressing toward a positive bovine dissatisfaction. Furthermore, we were sitting on the sweetest and most tender tufts of grass remaining. We courteously dismissed the peasant to go his way. His marked alacrity was quite welcome.

We lingered on the grass for a little while and I told Alfred my guesses. I elaborated them into the hazard that the poor man—he had not once turned to look back over his shoulder—might even then be fearing that the slight taste from the chocolate would turn him into a frog and his ox into a stork to eat him up. Or perhaps he might be in distress that he and his beast might grow smaller and smaller until they would disappear into thin air.

Alfred had been examining the faintness of the path. "I hope none of these things happen until the man gets over the hills to Narii. The hoof prints make an excellent trail," he said.

It was time to sling on our packs and follow. When we reached the next turn we could see the peasant's straw hat and the ox's straw bonnet bobbing along just over the bush tops. We maintained this distance without closing the gap. As Alfred had predicted, the hoof marks were useful. The path often grew so faint that it had no other resolute indication. We had been sure, without thought of other possibility, that the crest of the hill we were climbing would be the summit of the range. When we reached the crest we stood looking up at another peak rising from a shallow valley at our feet.

"Which way does the ox say to go?" I asked.

The hoof marks were there in the soft earth, but where our feet had stopped there they had stopped. They stopped as absolutely as if the peasant and his ox had been whisked away in a chariot to the sunset sky. The bushes were too low for concealment. There was no cave, nor hole in the earth.

If there be no such thing as magic, in the Japanese mountains at least, where did that man and his beast go? The disappearance was as complete as the most exacting enchanter could have desired. We found no answer to the riddle and the sun was sinking, adding the next question of how we were going to get out of the hills in the night time if we delayed for scientific investigation. We succumbed to expediency and took a five-mile-an-hour pace over such trail as we had left, guessing at the turns. When we finally reached the next crest, deep in the valley we could see Narii. Before descending the steep, dropping path, we sat down near a spring where the birds had come to drink. They were singing evening songs mightily. Bright wild flowers were scattered in the open spaces between the intense green of the fern patches. The world was lustily at peace.

When we did start we swung down the long hill almost at a run and in a half-hour reached the edge of the village to find Kenjirō sitting under a stone lantern in the temple yard. The evening peace had made us positive that this is the best of all possible worlds, but Kenjirō was entertaining a different idea. He looked exceedingly gloomy. We were impatient of any discontent. If he had said that men were starving for rice in the village beyond, the fitting answer would have seemed to us the historic words of the good queen: "Give them cake." Undoubtedly when the message about the starving peasants was brought to that Lady of France she was sitting under the shrubbery at Versailles, and the birds were singing, and it was springtime, and perhaps the fountains were playing. Impellingly she realized with an insight deeper than any historian has ever appreciated that upon such a glorious day, if there is any such thing as right or justice at all in this world, a certain amount of cake should be everybody's inalienable possession.

As it happened, Kenjirō's worry had nothing to do with altruistic sorrow for starving villagers, but existed from a lively interest in our own affairs. The town was very poor, he explained, a town come down in the world from ancient prosperity. Its neck was hung with the millstone of decayed graces and thinned blood. The inn was so old that it was senile. Kenjirō had established some excuse before entering the door for inspection which later allowed his rejection of the inn's hospitality, but it would never do for us in turn to venture in for a glance around. That would be needlessly raising the expectation of the ancient host. We would find, he suggested, that it would be only five or six or seven miles to the next village. As we had had twenty-five or more miles behind us and most of those had been along mountain paths, we were not so inevitably tempted at that hour of night to be particular in a choice of roofs as Kenjirō, who had come by train, was imagining.

The inn, in truth, was very old. By any law of survival chances the wandering wings should have burned to earth long ago. To greet us there were no smiling and chattering maids gathered behind a mistress. Instead, an old man and a very small girl, his granddaughter or more likely his great-granddaughter, met us in the dark entrance with protests that the house was unworthy of our presence. We hastily denied them their words. Kenjirō could employ the polite phrases of Japan. We impulsively, directly, and bluntly told them "no." It was not alone the pathos of the two figures which appealed. It was somewhat that their dignity had not surrendered to ruin, and it was somewhat a something else, indescribable, in the atmosphere that charmed.

We followed the master along a labyrinthine corridor. The soft wood planks of the floor had been polished to a deep reddish gleam under the bare feet of generations of hurrying *nee-sans*. He led us past inner courtyards to the farthest wing. Our room hung over the river at an elbow of the stream. Even with the *shōji* pushed wide open we were hidden completely from the eyes of the town by heavily leafed trees.

The mats on the floor had turned a dingy, mottled brown and black from their once light golden yellow, but they were clean. The sacred *kakemono* alcove still compelled its importance. It had been built in an age when the demand for its existence was the ardent faith of the builders rather than an architectural tradition. The room was about thirty-five feet long and fifteen feet deep, perhaps a little larger. The ceiling was proportionately high.

Kenjirō was still doubtful, not gloomily so, but from the knowledge that an inn is proved by its service. The host was kneeling, as immobile as a temple image, awaiting our orders. His skin was as bloodless as the vellum of the painting which hung behind him. His watchful eyes, however, were intensely bright in their deep sockets. Kenjirō began inquiries about dinner. The ancient bowed his head to the floor, drawing in his breath sharply against his teeth. Dinner was now being prepared for his family, he said, but it would be unworthy of his guests. The formal phrase of polite deprecation carried this truth, as Kenjirō discovered by

further questioning. It was not that the dinner was or was not worthy—
it was the failure of *quantity*. We should not have long to wait, said our
host, but food would have to be sent for.

As we sat in a circle planning what we should have, the old man smiled
and pointed to a patched square in the matting. Underneath the square, he
said, was a depression for holding bronze braziers. When the nobility, in
the old feudal times, had travelled the Nakasendō trail, this was the room
of honor that had been given to the *daimyō*. It had been often the custom
for the retainers of a *daimyō* themselves to prepare his dinner over the
braziers. Our sitting there, planning what we should have, had reminded
him of the dead past. His words came slowly as if between each word of
recollection his spirit journeyed back into the very maw of oblivion and
then had to return again to the world.

"Are the braziers still hidden there?" Kenjirō interrupted.

Yes, the braziers were under the floor or somewhere to be found.

Kenjirō turned to us and put us through a questioning until he
rediscovered the word "picnic" for his vocabulary. "That's what we will have,
a picnic, right here," he declared, and he turned back to the host to explain.
The old man almost gasped, at least approaching as near to such escape of
emotion as he probably ever had at the request of a guest.

"But you will then have to have a special waitress," he said. "My
granddaughter is indeed too young for that privilege." Always when he used
depreciatory adjectives about the child's unworthiness he failed lamentably
to harden his caressing tone. She was, however, as he had said, little older
than a baby. The services of a maid we should have to pay for, but, under
the spell of the conjuring up of the memories of those bygone revels in our
room, what cared we for saving our precious *yen*? We had become
reincarnations of the two-sworded swaggerers. We waved our arms grandil-
oquently.

"Tell him to send for fowls for the pot," we oratorically assailed Kenjirō.
"Let us mix rich sauces and warm the *sake*. And tell him to remember that
for us there can be but one choice—the maid to serve our dinner must be
the prettiest maid in all Narii."

I had not the slightest idea that Kenjirō would translate our exact words,
but I found later that such was his act.

Thus the mountain village of Narii faced a problem. Two foreigners, and a Japanese almost as alien as a foreigner, had appeared from nobody knew where, not preceded, it was true, by retainers as had been the travellers of old, but nevertheless demanded the old-time service with as much gusto as if they were accustomed to having what they wished. They had asked that the prettiest maid in all Narii be called to the inn to exercise the privilege of guarding the steaming rice box. It was obvious that there could be only one prettiest maid, and all Narii knew with one mind that the prettiest maid was the daughter of the Shinto priest. However, the daughter of a priest is not a likely candidate for service in an inn, even if the master has ever been a faithful devotee of the temple. Nevertheless there was the honor of the hospitality of Narii at stake. Messengers (or even appropriately, it might be said, heralds) were sent to explain the problem to the maid and her father, and to use, if necessary, the pressure of "the state demands."

Thus came Hana-*san* to the inn. (In all Japan there cannot be a prettier, a more bashful, or a more modest maiden.) Her eyes were downcast behind long black lashes. Her soft cheek flushed and paled—perhaps somewhat from the excitement of the adventure. Neither she nor her friends had ever seen one of that strange race, the foreigner. And, indeed, even a priest's daughter may think that to be chosen as the prettiest maid——!! Ah, her courage failed her to glance up and words would not come to her lips to answer their questions, but they did not seem to be so very predatory nor so very fearsome—and they were very hungry.

Two great bronze braziers had been filled with glowing charcoal. The foreigners and the outer-world Japanese who could speak their strange words were busily cooking the fowls, chopped into dice, and they were arguing about their respective talents and abilities, as do all amateur cooks. Perhaps she could now look up for an instant unobserved. No, a glance met her eyes and she felt hot blushes grow again on her cheek.

While they feasted and laughed she had to run many times to the kitchen for forgotten dishes. When she passed along the hall by the entrance to the street she was each time stopped and besieged by the questions of the gathered mob. (Some of those inquiring investigators had also gathered outside the wall of my bath an hour before. I had been suddenly aware of an eye at every crack and crevice of the boards as I was cautiously stepping into the superheated tub. There was not a sound, merely the glitter of their star-scattered eyes.)

The foreigners put sugar on their rice and one of them even put sugar in his tea. They handled their chopsticks so awkwardly that it was marvellous that they did not spill the rice grains on the matting. She thought of the twenty rules in etiquette for the proper and graceful use of chopsticks and she imagined that if there had been a ten score of rules they might have all been broken. At last the three feasters finished their mighty meal and stretched out on the cushions to smoke in deep contentment. She doubted whether they had even noticed that her superior *kimono* was not such as a maid of an inn would possess. After the feast her quick feet, in spotless white *tabi*, carried away the bowls and little tables. Then she sat down by the door to await any further clapping of hands.

The host came in, moving silently across the matting. He kneeled and bent his forehead to the floor. Before the meal he had himself arranged the flowers, in an old iron vase, to stand in the *kakemono* alcove. We tried to express our appreciation for the flowers and our admiration of the vase.

We asked him how old the inn was. It had been his father's before him, and his grandfather's before his father. Yes, in those days the Nakasendō had rivalled the Tōkaidō, and yearly, on the hastening to Edo to give obeisance to the *shōgun*, the great nobles of the northwest provinces with their armed retainers had had to pass through Narii. In the pride of their gifts to the *shōgun*, in their numbers, in their courage, they had never yielded place to the envoys from the great families of the South. This now forgotten inn had then been famous. Our room, overhanging the river, he repeated, had been only given to the *daimyō*. The *samurai* had crowded the other rooms. The inn had boasted a score, two score, of trained and pretty *nee-sans* to wait upon those fiery warriors. (The modern *geisha*, in many of her accomplishments, is daughter to the inn maidens of the feudal days who sang and danced and played musical instruments in addition to the graces of more domestic duties.) The inn had then rung with shouting and laughter, and sometimes the dawn of the morning start of the cavalcade found the retainers still sitting around the feast.

On the road to Edo their purses had hung full, but the great city always plunged both its hands into those purses filled from the rice taxes, and it was often quite another story—the return journey back to the provincial castles. No rare occurrence was it indeed, for some haughty *samurai* to declare in the morning that he could not pay his inn bill, however modest it might be. Upon one occasion a certain warrior had been forced to leave in pledge the first mistress of his heart—his sword. A *daimyō*, overlord of a province, could, of course, never be in debt to an innkeeper, although he might leave a gift for his host instead of money. When such eventuality as that arose the host would declare (wisely) that his hospitality had been unworthy of any remuneration and that he was a thousand times repaid by the magnificence of the gift.

Yes, went on the old man, once a noble upon leaving the door had caused a vase to be unwrapped from its encasements of one silken bag after another and had given it to the inn. The donor had written a poem of dedication with his own hand. The vase was shaped like a bottle and the inn had been called "The Bottle Inn" from that day, seventy years in the past. Our host, a youth on that day, had thought that the inn would ever be rich and renowned. He sighed. The tradition of its renown had faded and been forgotten in this age of railways. No longer did turbulent guests demand that the bottle be brought out and shown.

If his dramatic genius had been subtly leading us toward turbulence, we obeyed the pulling of the strings. We demanded to know whether the vase was still under his roof. Our host smiled. The sacred vase was hidden safely. Would we like to see it?

He returned, carrying an old wooden box. The great-granddaughter dragged the unredeemed sword after her. The well-worn scabbard of the sword was of mediocre, conventional design, but the blade had been forged by one of the famous sword makers. Kenjirō read the sword's origin from the characters carved in the steel. The old man slowly slipped the sword back into the scabbard, leaving us to ponder what might have been the tragic fate of the *rōnin* that he had never returned for his pledge.

No casket of precious metal can be so alluringly suggestive of trove as the simple, unpainted, pine boxes into which the Japanese put their treasures. A woven cord clasped down the lid of the box. The untying of it began the breathless ceremony. When the lid was lifted we saw the first silken wrapping, then came another, and another, and another. Some were of brocade, some were of faded plain color,——red, blue, or rose. Finally the drawing string of the last bag was pulled open and the old man lifted the bottle. It was of yellow pottery with a thick brown glaze overrunning the sides. The mouth of the vase was capped by a bronze and silver band carved with an irregular motif.

The trustee of the possession allowed us to pass it from hand to hand.

What was one of our reasons for being in Narii at that very moment? It was that our eyes were prying for those rarer treasures in Japan which may be sometimes gleaned "away from the beaten path." Unaccountable chance had led us to the inn. The old man was hopelessly beaten in his contest with poverty. I knew that he did not wish to sell, but if there should be the jingling of a few *yen*——was it likely that he could refuse? Our eyes were gleaming with desire. Surely, even if it were a venal sin to take away the bottle from The Bottle Inn the very greatness of the temptation would have brought its own special forgiveness. But because temptation and conscience can generally be argued around to our satisfaction, the gods have ironically added impulse as the third part of us. It must have been some such impulse which was the irrational lever which moved us to action. We soared to the heights. It was a superior endurance to any flight that it is likely either of us will ever attempt again. Truly such virtue is more regretted than gloried in. We did not take the bottle with us. It still functions in its environment, in harmony with its tradition. Taken away it could be only a superior vase with a history, an object of art. In that old inn it is a living part, an inspiration. In the forgotten village of Narii no numbered museum tag hangs around its neck.

The bottle dropped back into the brocade bag lined with faded crimson silk. Then the other wrappings, one by one, muffled it. It went into the box, the lid was fitted into place, and the cord was tied. Do we gain strength from resisting such temptation? The writers of the Holy Church of the Middle Ages said so. By refusing that bottle I merely gained exhaustion. This moment I am stifled by the dust of the ashes of that murdered passion. My conscience replies with no response. It has lost the vitality of recoil, and thus, if ever such time may come, I may yet glory in a greater vandalism, some supreme Hunnish act, and there will be no rasping regret.

The breezes up among the snows of the mountains came down into the valley for the night. Wherever they were going they seemed to be quite undetermined as to their path. They blow from every side and into every corner of the room by turn. Little by little, to escape the drafts, we had kept pushing along the wooden shutters until we were at length completely walled in. It was not possible to imagine that a few miles away, down on the rice plains, the millions were nudely stifling while we were going to bed to get warm. The daughter of the priest had been dragging layers of bedding to the door and, when we clapped our hands, she had innumerable mattresses for each of us. For once it was unnecessary to stretch the mosquito netting. There seemed to be nothing left but to blow out the lights and cry: "*O-yasumi nasai!*" to the retreating patter of her footsteps.

"What's the midget granddaughter waiting for?" I asked Kenjirō.

"She wants you to go to bed," he said from under his quilt.

I jumped into the soft centre of my mattresses as requested. Then the butterfly dropped on her knees and crept backward around our beds. Out of a box she was pouring a train of powder until she had us each enclosed in a magic circle.

"Why?" I demanded.

Kenjirō laughed at me.

"It's *nomi-yoke*," he said. "Insect powder—what do you say in America? Bug medicine?"

I insisted that I had not seen the sign of a bug or an insect or a flea or anything looking like a marauder.

"Of course not," Kenjirō stopped me as if I should have known better. "It's just courtesy to honored guests, to show you that they would wish to protect you if there were any. If there were crawlers," he concluded with some scorn, "do you suppose they'd make such an effort to call attention to the fact?"

That *bushidō* explanation satisfied Kenjirō but I was doubtful. For the sake of verification I carefully destroyed the integrity of the rampart around my bed by opening up passages through the powder. I was willing to display a few bites in the morning to prove the truth. I went to sleep dreaming about two-sworded *samurai* who looked like pinch bugs, and they were swaggering around a wall of insect powder. However, the morning proved that Kenjirō was quite correct. The delicate attention had been born of pure courtesy.

Ideals of a Samurai

In the morning we found great brass basins of water waiting for us in the sunny iris garden. One of the super-errors that a foreigner can make in a native inn is to ask to have the basins brought to his room. Such a request can be understood only as a perversion, or a barbarity. One reason why the houses and inns seem so clean is that they eliminate so many of the chances for their being otherwise. This defense might be added into the weighing when criticizing Japanese nudity at ablutions.

Breakfast was brought to us steaming under the lacquer covers of the bowls, but the priest's daughter was not holding the wooden ladle for the rice. It was a rather late hour when she had returned to her father's house, but the mothers and daughters of a Japanese home are accustomed to having their working hours overlap into the night. In subtlety we brazenly accused each other of having frightened the gentle *nee-san* into not returning. The truth was—as it afterwards came out—that we had each found opportunity to hint to the host's ear the night before that the maid's slumber by no means should be disturbed for our morning's start. Thus we each privately thought we knew the secret of her non-appearance, but just as we were tying on our shoes at the door a breathless message was brought by her small brother. She had overslept. It had not been our late hour which was responsible. The family of the Shinto priest had sat up almost until the first light in the East to listen to the wonder tale of their daughter who had endured such a singular and daring adventure.

The ancient host gave us presents and we gave him presents. We said our farewells at the door and then, after that, he and his granddaughter walked along with us half through the village. Finally we bowed our formal seven bows of farewell. When we reached the end of the street we turned and saw them still standing where we had left them.

The road led across a wide, flat valley. That morning there was a truly extraordinary phenomenon. The claret red of the sun flamed and danced against the snows of the mountain wall at our left. Finally our road broke up into a delta of small paths. The soft earth had been so cut into ruts by heavy carts that Kenjirō was forced to accede to the demands of the bicycle that it should be assisted and not ridden, but he did not surrender until the wheel had demonstrated its malevolence by pitching him a half-dozen times off the saddle. Thus we all walked along together. The villages were rather mean, with the air of having come down in the world. Some of the towns, in the days before machinery, had had special fame in the various handicrafts. One had been known for its hand-made wooden combs. Evidently there remain some conservatives who have not yet countenanced modern vulcanite innovations, as wooden combs were still being made for sale. Entire families, from grandparents to children, were the manufacturers, the factories their own homes. We bought a boxful for a few *sen*. In arriving at a selling price they must have valued their time in the manufacturing as a gratuitous contribution to the arts.

Every once in a while Alfred and I had had our pleasure in drawing the long bow of our imagination concerning the architectural reason for a certain peculiar type of house. A recurring example is to be found in nearly every village. These buildings are unusually substantial and the windows are always heavily barred and shuttered. They give a suggestion of descent from the castles of feudal days. As I said, we had employed our elaborate imagining over the mysterious buildings, but our guesses had never brought us anywhere near to the truth. Kenjirō explained that they are the houses of the pawnbrokers. Kenjirō is the son of a *samurai*. (He has the right to wear, if he wishes, the full number of crests on his formal *kimono*.) The artists who made the old color prints used to give to the eyes of the two-sworded *samurai* an expression of warlike ferocity. When Kenjirō spoke of the pawnbrokers his eyes glared, and I was sure that I detected his hand starting to reach for the sword that has now gone from his girdle. However, the ubiquitous bicycle just then swung around and entangled him, as a reminder, probably, that this is a new age, a mechanical and not a feudal one, and that a *samurai* no longer has the general and hearty acquiescence of law and society to proceed to direct action against the loathed money lender. The law of the land says today that the pawnbroker must be considered as a free and equal citizen, enjoying full rights under the mercy of the emperor. Nevertheless (as the bars and shutters of his windows show), the money lender still wisely believes in keeping his powder dry even in an age of enlightenment.

When we had extricated Kenjirō from the bicycle and we had all got going again, he explained why the pawnbroker is the most hated member of Japanese society. Here are some of the other remarks that Kenjirō made about pawnbrokers:

They are always rich. (He meant the Asiatic wealth,—hoards of gold, not a checking account at a bank.)

They are uncanny.

They lead isolated, unhappy lives.

They always have a beautiful daughter (one only) to fall heir to the riches.

This daughter dreams of noble lovers, but no Japanese, whatever his rank, be it noble, humble, or decayed (or, for that matter, no matter how much in debt he may be to her father), would ever throw away his pride to wed a pawnbroker's daughter. Thus she is left to grieve out her heart in the midst of her father's luxury.

A Japanese believes certain things patriotically. I know that Kenjirō does not believe these same things intellectually, for I was once rude enough to continue an argument until he capitulated intellectually—but for the love of country and the required loyalty to what should be, he also keeps to the beliefs which he should have as a Japanese. After all, juxtapositioned to such faith, mere intellectual judgment does seem lacking in vital fluid.

The hiatus in Kenjirō's Japanese life—the foreign period and influence— began when he was of the high school age and went to America. Thus, at the time when the mind is supposed to be most receptive, he was separated from the traditions and ethical customs of his homeland, and he made no return home until he had left his American university. A peculiar duality may come from such a training. It would be impossible otherwise, for instance, that one individual should really appreciate both a symphony orchestra and a *shamisen*, not so much from the angle of technical divergence in the use of notes, tones, and scales as in aesthetic comparison. To any human being with emotional sensitiveness and response, not possessing a dual personality, acknowledgment of the rights of the symphony would seem to preclude those of the *shamisen*.

I had lost my Japanese pipe. Those little iron bowls continue to be a most admirable luxury through all of the days that one is in the land of their invention. When the traveller leaves the shores of Japan he takes away with him packages of silken tobacco and his pipe, only to find that he never lights it again. The charm is broken when the circle is broken, and the circle, I suppose, is a unity when one is lying on the cushions of a balcony overlooking a garden, and a maid brings the charcoal *hibachi* and a pot of tea. You touch the bowl of the pipe to the fire and then—three puffs and a half. You knock the ash into a bamboo cup. Perhaps the maid refills the pipe, touches it to the charcoal, and hands it to you again.

Ordinarily these pipes are sold everywhere, but at Narii we could not find them. When we were walking into Shiojiri I asked Kenjirō to help me keep an eye on the shops as we passed. After a time he said: "Here we are. Here's a one-price store."

We had not come upon just such a shop before. While the stock and the arrangement was purely native, the atmosphere of the place was distinctly un-Japanese. A little of everything was for sale, but instead of the selling being a social ceremony, the shopkeeper and his wife and his sons and his daughters were expeditious clerks and not hosts. The entering customer asked for what he wished to see, and a price tag told him the cost. That was the beginning and the end of any bargaining.

In the conventional shop the buyer sits down leisurely, after removing his *geta*, and perhaps has a cup of tea. If an ordinary utility is wished, the negotiating is necessarily devoid of much opportunity for extended approach, consideration, and conclusion, but it is always to be remembered that our idea of what is a waste of time may be the Japanese idea of a valuably used moment. The little shops have no opening and closing hours. Literally, there is all the time there is. The clerk does not sell eight, nine, or ten hours of his day to his employer. He sells all of it. As it is impossible to keep at high pressure for maybe twenty hours of the twenty-four (and twenty hours is not an exaggeration in some instances) nature's insistence for rest has to come out of the working day. The fact that the workers are not awaiting the striking of a clock for their liberty, but are more or less taking it as it comes, accounts for what is often a mystery to travellers, the easy gaiety of a busy Japanese street. Workmen put down their tools and stop for a visit; the shopkeeper chats indefinitely with a customer; the maids at the inns have plenty of time to light pipes for the guests and pour tea. Our idea is that the individual's liberty begins at the sharp demarcation of the hour which ceases to belong to the employer. After the wanderer has lived for a time in the midst of the Oriental system, the impression comes that time is a continuous flow and that it is not a succession of intervals as it is with us. The people of the East have even found a counteracting thrust to oppose the tyranny of the railroad schedule. By arriving at the station indefinitely early they can show their contempt for definite departures.

While we were buying my new twelve-*sen* pipe in the Shiojiri one-price store, Kenjirō commented with obvious emphasis several times that he was pleased that the prices were so carefully marked on the tags. As smoking may at any time become a ceremony, I spent many minutes in my selection, and through these minutes Kenjirō kept dropping his pointed comments, but I stored away the impression of his satisfaction over the price tags to be asked about later. An appropriate time did not come for several days. An hour came when we were lounging on an inn balcony in the soft night air.

It seemed that our method of shopping was the disturbing pressure against Kenjirō's peace of mind. We two foreigners undoubtedly had many flaws which came to light under the wear of intimate association, but it was this one which at last drove Kenjirō to the verge where he had to unburden his feelings. In the curio shops, or wherever we were making purchases, when we came upon something that interested us, we immediately asked: "How much?" It had been natural, when Kenjirō was with us, to rely upon him to interpret rather than to employ our own cumbrous methods of transmitting ideas. As soon as we received an intimation of the bargain price we proceeded to the bargaining and continued until we arrived at what was presumably the lowest compromise of the shopkeeper. Kenjirō had also noticed that we sometimes put off deciding whether we really wished to purchase until we discovered the eventual price. We quite reversed the ceremonial purchase making enacted by a Japanese gentleman. As Kenjirō witnessed it, the difference was meaningful. The Japanese collector looks first of all at an object to see whether it merits his attention. If it does, there follows an extended conversation about its intrinsic excellence. Every question as to artistic value, authenticity, age, workmanship, uniqueness—these are all settled before a word about the price arises. If the object does not equal his demands of it, the collector departs without inquiry about the money value—for why should he be interested in the cost of an article if not in the article itself?

Kenjirō shook his head sadly. "You always ask right away: 'How much?'" he said. "That sounds very mercenary to us. It looks as if you were more interested in cheapness than quality."

We had not suspected that Kenjirō was writhing when, under the pressure of our Occidental impetus, he had been asking for us the questions of price. As a matter of fact, be it to his credit and our discredit, despite the simplification of his quick interpreting against our imperfect use of the few words that we did know, when it came to the detail of price our efforts often seemed to be able to effect a more extraordinary drop from the original quotation than when such arguing was put off until all other details were settled. It is true that the merchants who have really fine things will not show nor sell their best to customers whose appreciation they doubt, but it may also be true that as far as we did have appreciation, we made up our minds more quickly than does the Japanese collector, and thus the stages of consideration which Kenjirō missed were not so much lacking as they were abbreviated.

The standards of the *samurai* when he goes forth to make purchases should not be confused as being an index to the methods of modern Japan in attacking the world's markets. In such trading there is no nation which is more intent upon giving the customer what the customer thinks he wants, and price and profit are sufficiently an affair of cold business to be safely refrigerated against any germs of sentimentalism. Kenjirō was speaking as the son of the civilization which flowered in the feudal days. Whatever that civilization was, it was not commercial. In that old regime the shopkeeper was only a shopkeeper, and a discussion of ethics in trade occupied little space in the code of honor of the nation. When Kenjirō's fathers stopped to buy a fan or a bronze or a roll of brocade or sandals for their feet, or whatever it might be that they wished, bargaining stopped as soon as they reached the end of their patience—and they were most impatient warriors. They might arrogantly pay what was asked, or, if their patience was too far gone, they might lop off the head of the obdurate merchant. The last probability had a tendency to keep prices fairly near to an equitable level when the two-sworded men were purchasers.

It is not an appreciated trait in the modern world to have contempt for money. Japan's nobility, when the *shōgun* ruled, had sincere contempt for money. There is something dramatic, even noble, in having such a contempt, but it must be said that it is a much easier possession to maintain if behind it the possessors have the inalienable ownership of their landed estates. The descendants of the ancient orders in Japan do not own the land today and, examining their position in the cold light of fact, their contempt for any consideration of things commercial is the sign-board finger pointing to their eventual elimination. It was the miracle of all time when those noble families responded to the necessity of the new order, forced upon Japan by the outside world, and gave up their feudal right to the land to the emperor for a more democratic distribution. They not only surrendered their land in response to the emperor's edict, but they metamorphosed their sons into statesmen to help carry through the ideal. Their children went to foreign lands and labored at menial tasks to learn the ways of the *seiyō-jin*. Returning home they recognized that the standards both of commerce and ordinary trade had to be raised. Their encouragement to their country to proceed along new lines was practical and effective. Nevertheless, few were the sons of the nobility who themselves entered the world of commerce. Rather was it that they encouraged a middle class to rise. Even with no longer a perpetuation of power through landed estates, the old aristocracy has so far continued to exert the preponderating influence in national leadership. Can they continue to cherish a contempt of money and at the same time withstand the power of the new commercial class which is becoming richer every year while they are becoming poorer? Can they prove that, even in this age, honor and loyalty need not have to go hand in hand with money, and that poverty, second only to death, is not the great leveller?

Curiously, indeed, the abandon which comes from contempt for wealth by this class in Japan has had a bullish effect in one small department of world trade. Westerners first thought of Japan as a nation so given over to aestheticism that it used its hours in creating beautiful works of art and then admiring them. In those early days examples of their highest achievement in art were to be found at incredibly low prices. For a decade or two after its ports were forced open by the foreigner, the country was absorbed in adjusting itself to meet conditions unique to its traditions. It was a revolution which had to endure the strain of the uncompromising lavishness of war without the excitement of war. In such a period "priceless" art objects had their price. Those objects of art had been so intimately associated with the calm of the old order in its social and religious system that when that order gave ground the Japanese disregarded such possessions. It was then that gold lacquer boxes were either sold for a sum equal to the mere salvage of the gold or else melted in the furnace.

Those first years of readjustment presented the glorious days for the foreign collector. Then came reaction. To their own bewilderment the Japanese awoke to find that their love for the beautiful had not been merely an appendage of the feudal system. They began to compete for their own treasures. Prices began to advance to the mystification of the foreign buyers. The Japanese aristocrats were entering into collecting with that abandon which can exist only through sincere contempt for money. Thus it is that very few fine things now come out of Japan. Japan is poor, desperately poor, and it would seem that our millionaires should easily outbid them, but to a mind commercially trained, eventually there enters a consideration of price. To the son of the old Japanese nobility there is no such consideration except the limit of his purse. I heard the story of a young nobleman who desired a certain Korean antique. His wealth was about six hundred thousand *yen*. Like the Roman youth who shook dice, hazarding himself to become the slave of his opponent should he lose, this young Japanese entered the bidding until it was his last *yen* which bought the antiquity. The dilettante does not bid successfully against that spirit.

Many Queries

In abrupt change as we neared Shiojiri the people grew more prosperous and more smiling. One housewife along the way was busy with a gigantic baking in the sun. I have forgotten just what she said the small cakes were which she was patting out so expeditiously by the hundred. Her hands coquettishly fell into error in her routine when we wished her good-day. She had an adventurous spirit behind the work-a-day masque of her face. Inordinate questioners as we could generally prove ourselves, it was she who took and kept the lead in every kind of interrogation. She wanted to know all about the great world over the ridge of mountains which stopped her sight. She followed this questioning with an exposition of facts which she already knew about foreigners. She could be quite sure, she said, that the information which she had previously collected through gossip had in no way been adulterated by exaggeration. The proof was that we looked exactly as she had hitherto imagined foreigners. This comment was more interesting than flattering. Her anecdotes about foreigners were fluently parallel to the tales about pagans which I used to hear as a child from the cook when she returned from her missionary circle.

I asked our hostess if she would let me take her picture. My hesitation in asking was an unnecessary contribution to the proceedings. She was much pleased. She patted down her hair, rubbed her cheeks with a pale blue towel until they were rosy red, and then dusted her hands and arms with rice powder. After that she ran into the house to reappear without her trousers. Kenjirō told her quickly that foreigners are greatly shocked to see women in skirts. We appropriately pretended to be unseeing long enough for the hasty redonning of the discarded trousers and then the camera clicked.

Foreigners, particularly missionaries, are by no means unknown in the quarter of Shiojiri built around the railway station. The town is a rather important junction. At the new inn the servants who met us at the door told us that they knew just what the foreigner likes. We in our obstinacy refused to like what the foreigners who had come before us had said that they liked. It was one of the least happy of all our rests.

The service in the shiny new inn had lost the spontaneity, the not-to-be-imitated bloom of the *yadoya* which makes each guest believe that he is the most honored. It had resolved into the inevitable mortification which comes from trying to please two masters. When they asked whether we wished native dishes or foreign dishes for dinner, we kept insisting that we wished Japanese fare, but the inn could not shake itself free from compromises and we had a native dinner cooked after some imagined foreign style. Just as we would have had a semblance of a foreign dinner cooked in the native pots if we had consented to act our proper parts as *seiyō-jin*. The trouble with such in-between places is not so much that they are jerry-built or that the ignorance of *why* is naturally followed by an ignorance of *how*, but that something essentially vital has been abstracted: the fire has gone, and the result is a listless lassitude.

Across the street was the entrance to another inn, with an electric sign at the gate and with two rows of paper lanterns hanging over the path. While we were taking a walk and looking in at the shops Kenjirō picked up the information from someone that the rival establishment to ours was half inn, half *geisha* house, that the maids, in fact, were country *geisha*. Every *geisha* must have a *geisha's* ticket from the government to follow her vocation of innocent amusing. All *geisha* are not innocent, but says the government, if they are not they must possess another license. Through its varieties and grade of licenses the government relies largely upon maintaining order. Thus, much of the work of the police is devoted to social regulation to prevent disorder rather than to the otherwise necessity of curbing it after it breaks forth. In any social system, whether the general scheme reaches out for the ideal or not, if the cogs fit in smoothly enough to work at all, the logical conclusion reads that the better the machine runs the more nearly have the everyday, actual wishes of the people been satisfied. In Japan the social regulations and the demands of the popular moral standard appear to mesh without much friction. This does not mean that the social problem has been solved, but it does mean that the compromise has measurably been made with eyes open and thus some evils have been successfully eliminated.

The *geisha* tea-houses have their special licenses, and inns have special licenses. While many combinations of licenses are possible, it is contrary to custom to issue a permit to a *geisha* house to have all the privileges of an inn. Kenjirō thought that there might be licenses of that sort issued in the smaller provincial towns such as Shiojiri. Whatever the facts were, such a combination license would seem to be contrary to the usual intent of the regulations. The government proceeds about its business of regulation without much sentiment, but it does seek by its very system of labelling to secure to the innocent the assurance of travelling through the kingdom without unwittingly having to come into contact with vice. The traveller is supposed to be able to go to an inn without having to inquire whether it is also a questionable tea-house.

It might seem that the easiest way to have found out what was the exact status of the inn across the street would have been to have walked there and asked. Kenjirō, however, was lukewarm for any such investigation. I discovered in this mood of Kenjirō's cosmos a trait more interesting than the entire subject of licenses. The intuition came suddenly in a wholeness. This trait might have been called patriotic, a patriotism so very broad that in the first inkling it seemed narrow. He had a deep desire that we should understand Japanese ideals, and his process of thought was that while he believed that to understand Japan we must see everything, nevertheless at all times there should be a certain normality in the seeing. As he explained, many Japanese customs and modes of thought, puzzling at first, are quite comprehensible when the entire fabric is examined. He did not wish to have certain squares of the embroidery held up to be criticized without the offset of properly contrasting squares. Naturally his own impetus often carried him a little beyond that normal into looking for the bright and golden patches and ignoring the dull ones. I think he was theoretically right, but most of us have a childish overconfidence in our maturity and we do not wish to have it doubted that we are capable observers even of the abnormal.

Experience has not trained us to follow, even if we wished, an idealized instruction. Thus I am afraid that Alfred and I remained recalcitrant observers most of the time and in our own way used our philosophical microscopes in a grandiose attempt to disintegrate the atom and conclude the infinite.

It is true that the most balanced mind can be poisoned by an impression. We are sensitized to light and shade. The traveller who goes to one of the great capitals of the world and endures as his first impression a visit to the dregs of the underworld forever finds the darkness of that shadow over his concept of all else. This comparison indeed puts a superlative exaggeration upon Kenjirō's not wishing to go to the inn-tea-house across the street. Just because I happened to glean something of his attitude about our excursion as a whole from that particular incident did not mean that he was attaching particular importance to it. The subject was dropped and as we were all tired, we went to bed, and allowed the double row of paper lanterns to swing on in the breeze without our three figures casting shadows on the path beneath, and the question that interested me about what sort of a license had been issued there was never settled.

The next morning Alfred and I were off at an early hour, leaving Kenjirō to follow on the bicycle. The heavy dew had clotted the dust and the cobwebs were glistening. It was so cold that we fell into our fastest gait, but perversely the town kept creating some new and picturesque allurement to slow our stride at almost every pace. Many of the most important houses had the dignity of villas. I suppose the owners of those houses look upon the town's activity as a railway junction not as a crowning glory but as a deplorable disturbance. Before the railroad was dreamed of, Japan's aristocracy had cherished that particular hillside overlooking the view of the valley with the snow ridges beyond. The prosperous shopkeeping streets were busy even at our early hour. Boys and girls were flushing the pavements, fanning out the water from wooden dippers. The fathers were taking down the shutters, and the mothers were giving indiscriminate directions while they rubbed their eyes and pulled their kimono straight. Many greeted us with a cheery "O-hayō."

At the edge of the town a temple gate stood invitingly open and we entered the garden and crossed a diminutive bridge to an island. We sat down to listen to the birds, admire the butterflies, and watch the gold and silver fish bob out of the water. The silent temple, hidden in the shadows of the trees, was built after the noble lines of the Kyoto tradition and may have been contemporary with that era. We were waiting for Kenjirō. We knew that we had several intricate turnings before we should come to our mountain road to Kami-Suwa, and we were indulging ourselves that morning in unwonted conservatism over the possibility of a mistake. We sat for some time waiting to hear the jangling of the bicycle bell, but as no such sound came from the distance and as the sun had not warmed the air, we decided to take the most attractive turns that came, right or wrong.

The street that intrigued our fancy wound delightfully between large country houses. While there was nothing except the trees and a certain pervading atmosphere to suggest the English country, nevertheless there was the instinctive feeling that within those screened, luxurious houses the sleeping families were quality folk, a class never forgetting that their position carries responsibilities, duties, and privileges. To meet a panting coolie dragging a *rikisha* along an English lane would strike one not only as strange but ridiculous. To have seen a gate open that morning in the outskirts of Shiojiri and to have had a shining British dogcart swing out into the road atop the heels of a cob would have seemed neither incongruous nor absurd. That's the reward the English achieve from their devout worship of the correct. In any corner of the globe when the beholder finds people getting serious about form, his mind immediately institutes a comparison with the British standard.

We walked on into a maze of hills. In the age of chaos the mountain range had tried to turn to the south but, meeting some powerful opposition, had been rolled back over on itself. When we came to the meeting of a half-dozen crooked paths there was no possible guess for our direction. We sat down in the sun for a few minutes, allowing that much time to good fortune to send us help, if the god of luck should so wish to aid, before attempting anything on our own initiative. We were sent two farmers whom we almost lost through their sudden surprise upon seeing us spring up out of the bowels of the earth. However, they had only been startled, and they did not think we were transformed demons. They entered into an energetic discussion of our route, insisting that we take the trail which was the faintest of all and which seemingly wandered off in the most irresponsible way. It first crossed a footbridge over the stream. One of the men dug a map in the dust with his toe. We finally parted with bows and protestations of gratitude and they stood in the valley and directed us on our climb as long as we could see them. Then they waved a final adieu and started on their own path.

It was decidedly a shortcut they had disclosed. When we were on a summit we discovered Kenjirō far below wheeling over the long valley road and undoubtedly wondering why he did not overtake us. Probably a *rikisha* could get through those hills by keeping to the lower paths, but neither our generation nor that of our children's children will find those narrow trails made over into motor highways. For generations the tramper will have his "unspoiled" Japan. It is true that east to west the mountains have been pierced by two lines of railway and the foot trails sometimes cross the steel, but now that the railroads have been built the trains running through the valleys and plunging into the tunnels seem to be as alien to, as outside the lives of the mountain folk, and as little considered in their existence as the invisible messages hastening along the telegraph wires. Japan has been opened to the world and science has brought an infinite change to the Japan that we think of, but over those mountain paths long lines of coolies stagger with their loads of merchandise as they did in the days before wheels were invented. Many of the coolies are women and girls. Over the steep miles the backs of the little girls are bent under chests which, thrown to the ground, would be large enough for playhouses. I know nowhere else in the world where faces do not grow stolid and stupid under such strain, but these women and little girls often turn upon you faces not only pretty but even strangely beautiful as they raise their heads for a quick glance. Their wistful eyes ask unanswerable questions. You feel as if they were eternally pondering the *why*.

I do not mean that such glimpses can bring more than a merest intuition of a people's attitude toward life. Such a gossamer web of intuition is a personal speculation, but it may be not too presumptuous for foreign eyes to make a diagnostic examination of physical characteristics and to believe that some truth may be reached from accumulated observations. While the Japanese nation is old in history and civilization, and while time's hammer has made the people as nearly homogeneous as is synthetically possible, nevertheless their predominant physical characteristic is that as a race they are youthful in vitality. The coolie bends his shoulders to as heavy a load as he can carry, but also does the coolie of Southern India. Existence seems to offer not much more in prizes to one than the other beyond the promise of the opportunity to labour day after day until death, but in the Indian's face one reads that the draught of unquestioning acceptance of fate was drunk by his fathers ages ago. That strong arch of the Japanese jaw means *future*. The struggle among nations for dictatorship may end in competition's giving the award to the people having the best teeth.

We passed two or three lonely, terraced farms where the earth was being coaxed and coddled not to run away, but through most of the hours of the climb the mountain sides were a forest reservation serving as a reservoir to save the water of the streams for the lower valleys. When we came to a spring gushing from the hill we drank, an action which is sternly warned against, and probably with absolute justification. However, with a four-mile-an-hour pace under the July sun thirst becomes positive. We mixed into the clear water, against any lurking germs, the antidote of deciding to consider ourselves immune. After a time our trail brought us down again into the valley, and it was not until then that Kenjirō caught up with us although he had been circling around the base of the hills at full speed. He found us locked in a bargaining struggle with a gooseberry peddler. The man was carrying his produce in a bucket swung at one end of a yoke across his shoulders, and his pensive little daughter was balancing the load by sitting in the other bucket. Our first advances had unutterably confused his wits, beginning with the logical wonderment why two pedestrians miles from any town should wish to buy green gooseberries. As the bargaining continued his puzzlement was relieved by a sudden lightning suspicion. We were not buying gooseberries, we were trying to buy his daughter! It seemed so discourteous to rob him of his hard thought out solution that I urged Alfred strongly to adopt the child and carry her off in his rucksack. It was just then that Kenjirō arrived. He jerked the demon bicycle to a stop and vaulted to the ground. At first he was as uncomprehending of why we wished to load up with green gooseberries as had been the peddler, but that night he fully acknowledged the value of our whim when the berries, stewed in sugar, stood before him.

I had taken the camera out of my pack but the man was most suspicious of it. We compromised that I should stand up and show just what taking a picture was. As soon as I made the demonstration his quick refusal against such devil's work followed. Quite by chance the camera had clicked during the demonstration.

April-like showers had been tumbling upon us now and again without disturbing the sunshine. We had one more long climb and then found ourselves with Lake Suwa far below. The town of Kami-Suwa rested on the farther shore of the lake in a narrow line of houses. Despite the rain flurries the day seemed very clear, but we did not have the famous first view of Fuji-*san* that sometimes gloriously greets the traveller when he stands, as did we, suddenly on the heights above the lake. On those rare days the mountain rises against the blue sky, the vista coming through a sharp gap in the granite hills, and casts its image on the grey-blue waters. This is the view from the north. The conventional view is from the south, but the sacred mountain lessens never in beauty as the worshipper circles the paths about its base, north, south, east, or west. Like a glorious and beautiful soul, its moods change while it changes not.

Is it idolatrous to worship Fuji-*san*? Is it pagan to love its beauty, to feel one's spirit freed for a brief moment, forgetful of experience tugging at one's elbow, of caution, of fear, of expediency, of pride?

The Inn at Kami-Suwa

The railway train with its sly befuddling through the luxury of speed has picked the traveller's wallet. Cooped behind a smudged window, how can he sense the personality of the town he enters? One should stand in isolation on the heights above a city, and then follow down some path until within the streets one is absorbed by the throbbing life. (Hobo Jack, *ipse dixit*. And is this not true?)

To appreciate Kami-Suwa's surcharge of culture, prosperity, and importance, the reader should think of a small city in Kansas (one of those temperate, prosperous, ideal cities of which one has a vividly exact idea without the proof or disproof from having visited it). I say this, knowing only the standardized impression of those ideal cities, but often a common, standardized impression may be more expeditious, not to say more valuable, or even more truthful, to communicate a comparison than the truth itself. Thus, by such a comparison let Kami-Suwa be known.

The Kami-Suwa streets are filled with good citizens. The shops are superior, the town has "as fine a school system as you could find anywhere." The temple is "well supported," and there are not any very poor people. Also the town has famous hot springs and famous views. In the age when Nature was distributing her gifts she favored Suwa with excessive partiality, in anticipation, perhaps, of the future births of today's appreciative, virtuous, honest, and industrious Kami-Suwans.

We had had a good report of a certain inn in the town and, after we reached the path around the shore, Kenjirō went ahead on the bicycle to prepare the way. The machine's parts were working together with remarkable smoothness that day, perhaps because its superfluous temper had been cooled down through its having been left out in a short, hard beating rain while we were taking refuge under a tree. We promised Kenjirō to hurry, but we did not. The mountains overhanging the lake were responsible in the beginning for our forgetting our word, but we augmented that beginning by finding some cause for a violent argument, one of those tempestuous discussions which gain their heat from the insidious conceding of small points. An obstinate, unyielding opponent who stays put is a far more satisfactory antagonist. We were well into the town before we discovered that we were hemmed in by houses. The interruption which opened our eyes was a polite pulling at our sleeves. One waylayer, out of the many who had surrounded us, had cast away in despair the usual Japanese respect for not touching the person.

Why our entry had created such excess of excitement we could not imagine. We had grown *blasé* in our role of being interesting exhibits. One may even grow so accustomed to having an interest taken in every detail that a lack of acknowledgment of curiosity seems the abnormal. This time mere curiosity did not appear to be the factor. Each waylayer was trying to speak. In the confusion I could not catch one familiar word. I knew most of the names that are sometimes cried at foreigners in the port cities, but there was nothing hostile in the present attack. As a sedative I tried to ask the way to the inn but my simple question increased the babel. We had no answer that we could understand. We had been smiling and bearing the mystery, and there was no choice but to continue so doing. Every shopkeeper in the street was apparently out now, helping to gesticulate if not to add words. We had continued walking and we came to an open space. All the brown hands simultaneously pointed in a dramatic sweep across a swampy field. On the roof of a large, new building stood Hori Kenjirō. He had changed into a *yukata* which he was modestly trying to hold around him in the freshening breeze and at the same time to wave a huge white sheet with all the energy of his other wiry arm.

When we reached the door Kenjirō had come down from the roof. He was very expeditious in his instructions to the servants and our shoes were off and we were in our room before we had a chance to ask a question.

"Now that we're *settled*———" Kenjirō began with a slight accent on the "settled." He then hesitated.

"Yes?" we inquired.

"Oh, I was just going to ask whether you wouldn't rather dry your clothes and take a bath before we go exploring around the town."

As Alfred had been answering that question by hanging up his wet clothes and getting into a cotton *yukata*, it did not seem to require argument.

"Is the bath ready?" he asked.

"It's always ready—natural hot springs," Kenjirō answered.

I stacked up some cushions and stretched out in comfort along the balcony. I sipped tea and smoked until I was sure Alfred would not be returning for something forgotten. I had been suspecting that Kenjirō's nonchalance had clay feet.

"Hori-*san*," I asked, "what did you say was the name of this inn?"

Alfred was always off to the bath as soon as his feet were inside an inn. This time I had marvelled that the habit was so strong that he could put off attempting to solve the mystery of our reception, especially as Kenjirō's naive casualness suggested that he knew the kernel of the mystery.

"It's a new inn. Very good, don't you think?" Kenjirō answered my question.

"What is the secret?" I demanded. It was evidently very dark and if the facts had to be modified in the telling, I thought that perhaps they might come forth less modified for me than for Alfred. The other inn had been one of our few planned quests. "Why didn't we go to the other inn?"

It may have been most unfair to use such a direct method of questioning, especially the distressing, bee-line "hurry-up." I was trading upon my being a foreigner from a land without the tradition of the proper ceremony of questions.

Yes, Kenjirō had visited the inn of which we had had the superior report. It was a most superior place. He paused. Then he vouchsafed the information that it was expensive. That was indeed a serious objection. He thought that the bill there might have come to three, four, or even five *yen* a day. That explanation should have been final enough for me. It was, in fact. I would have accepted it. I merely happened to ask whether he had looked at the rooms.

"Yes," he said, and then he suddenly threw discretion away. "And what do you think? *They had rocking-chairs and American bureaus in the rooms.*"

Poor Kenjirō! He had been having to listen to us inveigh in American exaggeration against the infamous inroads of modernity. I cannot imagine that he took our chants of hatred against innovations actually at their word value, but he had had much reason to become weary and bored from their repetition. He implied that his reason for leaving the other inn was for our aesthetic protection, but be it said he was wise in his own protection. There is not much doubt that if we had reached the presence of those rooms there would have been another merry-to-do of wild epithets against machine-made American export furniture bespoiling native simplicity for him to listen to. The tourist animal is truly a snobbish beast, and natives should occasionally be given dispensations for outright murder.

Once I was chatting over tall iced lemon squashes with a Japanese physician. In a surge of confidence, and also in burning curiosity, he told me about his trip to America. He had learned his English in Japan. While visiting a family whom he had known in his homeland, he met one of America's daughters who asked him to call. He was somewhat startled by the invitation but he remembered that he was not in the Orient. He described the conversation to me in awed phrases.

"She had a box of chocolates. 'Do you know,' she said, 'I am mad about chocolates, simply crazy.'

"I thought," he explained, "that she was confessing to a craving appetite and wished my assistance and advice. I imagined, then, that I knew the reason of my invitation. I was a physician from a foreign land and, as I must soon return to my own country, her secret with me would be as good as buried. I explained that I could do nothing for her without the full confidence of her father and mother. She took this natural suggestion as if it were meant to be humorous. When she had stopped laughing she told me that the Japanese are perfect dears and horribly cute. Then she asked me if I didn't love—— what was it she asked me that I loved? I forget. You see we Japanese have few words to express the affections and use those sparingly. And now," he leaned eagerly forward, "I want to ask you whether that young lady was charming?"

I tried to evade by asking him what was his idea of charming.

"That's just what I don't know. I was told that she was beautiful and charming. I could see that she was beautiful. Then I asked people what charming meant. They all told me something different."

"You can't define charming," I hazarded. "It's something different from a mere attribute. Foreigners always say that Japanese women are charming."

"Then she wasn't charming," he decided judicially.

Several times I have been so rash as to try to explain to men of other nations how much an ordinary American conversation should be discounted. I fear that they did not accept my formula but held to the extremes, either continuing to take us literally or not believing us at all.

After Kenjirō had discovered the untoward action of the first inn in adding rocking-chairs and bureaus to its equipment, he hurried down the street and warned the shopkeepers whom he could find to stop any two wandering *seiyō-jin* and direct their attention to the new inn. They must have been impressed that the affair was one of moment.

We heard Alfred, the feared critic of varnished, golden-oak-pine bureaus, coming up the stairs. A striped, blue *yukata* made in Japanese standard length somehow does not suggest dignity when worn by a more than six-foot foreigner with a beard, but Alfred came so solemnly across the mats in his bare feet that his ominous repression created its own aura of dignity. Something had happened, but he was not inviting questions.

Kenjirō started in turn for his bath. I remained on my cushions. I sat and sipped my tea. Alfred sat and sipped his tea. Kenjirō with his secret of the rocking-chair inn had not been impregnable to questions. Alfred was too dangerously calm. I waited.

He began by alluding to the excellence of the rooms we had. They were excellent, the best in the inn, being a part of an extra cupola story and giving a splendid view across the lake. Then he restated the known fact that the baths were served by natural hot springs. "The water comes pouring in through bamboo pipes," he said.

"Well," I spoke for the first time, "and then what happened?"

The honorable *seiyō-jin* drank another cup of tea.

"I got into the wrong bath," he said.

It was news that there could be any such thing as a wrong bath in a Japanese inn.

"You see," he continued, "the baths for the guests of the inn are just under us, but I didn't notice them when I walked by. When I got to the other end of the hall I found a large bath room. Those are the public baths, but I didn't know that then. There were several big tubs with the water tumbling in all the time from the pipes. There was nobody else there nor a sign of anybody. I made myself at home and was floating in one of the tubs when suddenly I heard a monstrous chattering out in the hall and then right into the room walked twenty girls. Maybe there were twice that many. I don't know. Well, I've called upon my practical philosophy to recognize the extenuating virtues of—ah—the natural simplicity of the traditional exposure of the Japanese bath—so to speak—its insecurity—as it were—but—but—h'm—yes— but this was too much."

I shouted.

He glared.

"I was just thinking——" I tried to say.

"I can see you are just thinking," he interrupted, "and I know what you are thinking. You are thinking what a great story this will be to tell when we get home. Believe me, if you ever do——"

"How could you ever imagine such treachery?" I wedged in.

"Well, and then what was I to do?" he demanded. "I couldn't jump out and run and I couldn't stay in that boiling water until I was cooked. I relied upon some instinct of feminine chivalry to give me a chance, but——"

I tried to be sympathetically consoling. "A very, very trying situation."

"Huh! They were all stepping in and they just naturally crowded me out. Of course they paid absolutely no attention——"

Kenjirō's step was on the stair. He came in and sat down and poured a cup of tea. Then he stretched out on his back and gazed innocently at the ceiling. "Doctor-*san*," he said, "you've settled a disputed point in Kami-Suwa and everybody's much obliged."

"What's that?"

"Well, there's been an argument for a long time whether *seiyō-jin* are white all over——"

The Guest of the Other Tower Room

Our tower wing of the inn at Kami-Suwa had required no architectural ingenuity in its design, but I do not remember ever having seen a Japanese building planned in the same way. The walls were open on the four sides and there was no *kakemono* alcove. The only approach was by a flight of stairs which belonged to it exclusively. We thus had an isolation most unusual. It mattered not the length and breadth of the space given us, our few possessions were always scattered over all the space available.

We heard steps on the stair and our hostess and a maid came up to us and bowed many times and brought many apologies. Half our space was to be taken away. This was only following the very equitable custom that a guest may have all of the extension of his floor until some other traveller must be accommodated, and then, presto! there are two rooms where one was before.

In a few minutes a double row of sliding doors (*fusuma*) had been pushed along the grooved slides in the floor from the head of the stairs, creating two complete rooms with a hallway between. The new guest, a woman, stood waiting to take possession. From the quality of her *kimono*, the refinement of her face, and the arrangement of her hair, we could judge that she was of superior rank. We questioned with some wonder why she was alone, but as it was extremely unlikely that that question or any other about her would be answered, the passing query was dismissed. However, it came about that we were to know one poignant chapter in that woman's life.

We went exploring to find the kitchen, there to deliver our gooseberries and our recipe. The maids and cooks stood and listened. We proceeded with our explanation until we reached the point where one more suppressed giggle on the part of the *nee-sans* might have burst forth into full hysterics. We released them in time by laughing ourselves and then left them to recover as best they could and to experiment with the stewing. Their irresponsible laughing for laughter's sake had infected us with the mood. We went filing back to our room. The guest of the second tower room was standing on the balcony at the head of the stairs. She had changed from her street *kimono*. Her eyes were shaded by her hand and she was looking searchingly down the road. As we walked by she stepped a little farther out on the narrow balcony but did not take her eyes from her quest.

The maid brought our dinner. It had been fourteen hours since breakfast and we had been tramping mountain paths, but without the sauce of appetite that dinner could have justified its existence. There were fish fresh from the mountain waters of the lake, and there were grilled eels, and there were strange vegetables with strange sauces. When the rice came we poured our stewed gooseberry juice over the bowl. The maid had left the *fusuma* pushed back when she carried off the tables downstairs. At that moment of our contentment I looked up to see the lonely watcher step back from the balcony. Her expression had changed to joyful expectancy and radiant relief and trust. She went to her room, then returned to the balcony, then ran again to her room. In a moment or two the round, sleepy maid stumbled up the stairs and whispered a message. The message again brought the woman to the head of the stairs and in a moment we could hear a man's step coming.

The greeting of affection in Japan is not a meeting of the lips. Whatever the proper cherishing expression may be, it cannot be such a casual acknowledgment as was that man's indifferent greeting in the inn at Kami-Suwa. A glance showed that he belonged to that new type which modern Japan has produced, the mobile, keen, aggressive, calculating, successful man of business and affairs. He was about thirty-five. Men of this new stamp are seldom met with in the provinces where the old order has changed so little but in Tokyo and the port cities their ideas are the predominant influence. Their aggression and ability have taken over the business and industries which the foreigner established. When one thinks of Old Japan one can believe that the thought action of this type of man by the very virtue of his being understood by us is enigma to those who still seek their inspiration in the ideals of the order that was.

"Well, I am here," he said. "You sent for me and I came."

The woman stood, making no answer.

"What's it all about?" he went on. "Your message was very mysterious. It cannot be that you have been so foolish—so unthinking—as absolutely to make a break with your husband?"

"You are tired from your trip," she said. "Come! Sit down! Your dinner is waiting to be brought."

He sat down and the woman clapped her hands for the maid. When the stumbling, awkward girl came the man changed the order and told the *nee-san* to bring *sake* first of all. He sat in silence until the hot rice wine came. He drank several of the small cups. Then the maid brought the lacquer tables with the dinner dishes. The man lifted up one or two covers and then suddenly jumped to his feet and declared that he was going to take a bath.

The maid led the way to the large room for baths which was just under our rooms. The woman sat before her untasted dinner. Soon there was a sound of laughing and chattering from below. There was the man's voice and the maid's laugh. Finally the woman arose, walked out into the hall, tentatively put a foot on the stair, then slowly walked down. She waited outside the sliding paper door. The maid had committed no breach against custom in lingering idly after carrying in towels and brushes. It was for no personal bitterness against the stupid maid that tears had gathered in the woman's eyes. There was nothing vulgar in the words of the bantering chatter she heard. It was the fact that the man was accepting the moment so carelessly, so unfeelingly for her anguish, knowing as he must unquestionably that every word of his indifferent greeting to her had carried a torturing thrust of pain.

The dinner was brought up again, warmed over. We heard the order for another bottle of *sake*. We could not escape hearing through the paper wall. We had intended taking a walk but a misty rain had come down. The mosquitoes arose from the beaches of the lake. We sent for the maid and asked for the beds and mosquito netting. In the meantime Kenjirō and I were tempted into taking another luxurious sinking into the hot baths. Alfred had turned out the light before we came back. In the darkness we crawled carefully under the omnibus netting and I went to sleep immediately. I awoke in about an hour. The misty rain had been blown away and the moon was shining so clearly that when I turned over I could see that Kenjirō's eyes were wide open. I heard the maid, stumbling as always, come up the stairs with another bottle of *sake*. I asked Kenjirō whether he had been asleep. He said that he had not, that after the woman had begun talking she had not stopped. I could hear her low, ceaseless tones. The man was smoking one pipe after another. He would knock out the ash against the brazier—four staccato raps—then there would be a pause for the three or four puffs from the refilled pipe, and then the staccato raps again.

"If we are ever going to get to sleep," said Kenjirō, "we'll have to complain to the mistress. Guests haven't any right to keep other guests awake."

"Why wouldn't it be better to make some such suggestion to them without calling in the mistress?" I asked.

Kenjirō shook his head. That was not the way. However, we delayed sending for the inn mistress. Kenjirō translated some of the conversation that he had heard before I woke up. The woman had that morning left her home and her husband. She had sent a message to the man now in the room with her, but her news had evidently been one of his least desired wishes. Before he sank into the silence of tobacco and *sake* he had said his disapproval.

"I thought you had more sense than to do anything so absurd, so almost final. Don't you see that it will be almost impossible for you to go back now? How will you make any explanation that he can accept?"

"But," she interrupted, "I came to you as you have so often said that you wished I could. That was the only way I could be even a little bit fair to him—to leave his house."

"Everything was all right as it was."

"No! No! I could not live that way."

"I can't see why. I don't see it. Now you've pretty nearly ruined both of us. However, we've got to think of some way for you to go back."

"But I can't. I've lost the possibility of that. If I had not thought you wished me, I might not have come to you, but I could not stay there."

"That's foolishness. Anyhow, you can go to your own family, and when he finds that is where you are, he'll want you to come back."

Her mind was dully grasping that here, with this man, she had no refuge, but her heart would not believe.

"I wished to make it complete," she repeated. "I wanted to give up everything for you."

What folly, what sheer childish folly, he told her, that she had listened seriously to his idle, passing phrases. Why, always, she must have known that he was merely answering her vanity. Any woman should have known and accepted that.

The ceaseless words and the staccato rapping of the pipe continued. We dismissed from our minds any intention of sending for the mistress, but not from prying curiosity. Our sleeping, or our not sleeping, was not of importance. In merciful pity (at least as we thought) for the woman, we knew that that contest must be settled as it was being settled. "But," Kenjirō whispered, "it would be a mighty big satisfaction to mix in a little physical argument."

"No one at this inn knows who I am," the man continued. "No one has any idea that you have more than the slightest acquaintanceship with me. No one would ever be convinced that you ran away to meet me."

She ceased the argument that she had come to him in willing sacrifice of all else—the supreme gift of her love for him. She began to plead. He did not answer. His pipe struck against the brazier and now and again the maid brought *sake*. Once she began to weep hysterically but this surrender to her agony was only for a short moment.

It was now almost morning. The rapping of the pipe stopped. The man got to his feet somewhat noisily. Passionately and despairingly the woman begged him not to leave her. Then as suddenly she ceased all words and said nothing as he made his preparations for going, nor did she call after him when he left her. Her unbeating breast imprisoned her breath through one last moment of hope. The spark of faith died but the torture of life remained, and her breath was released in a long, low moan. Until morning broke she sobbed, lying there on the floor.

She had not pushed back the wall panel which the man had left open. When we went below to our baths she drew in her outstretched arm which still reached gropingly into the narrow passageway. She dressed before we returned. We met her on the stairs. She started to cover her face with her *kimono* sleeve, and then, listlessly, dropped her arm.

"Where will she go?" I asked Kenjirō.

Kenjirō did not know. In the old regime, he explained, when a woman of the aristocracy left her husband she went to her family, but it had been only under extreme duress that a woman would leave her husband. There is much talk today in Japan that the social institutions are crumbling. One is told that the "new woman" movement is a result of the crumbling of the old order. And again one is told that the crumbling has come from the new woman movement. These latter critics say that so many women are leaving their homes that if any proper discipline is to be retained and maintained, the tradition that a woman's own family may receive her into their house must be uncompromisingly discouraged as a declaration of warning to others.

Kenjirō, himself, now that the tragedy had ceased to be so present, was somewhat inclined to look upon the history of the night in its relation to collective society rather than as the drama of two individuals. A Japanese instinctively regards a family as a family, and not as a collection of units. Loyalty is the basic idea of that philosophy and not the importance of the individual soul.

"There is one thing quite sure," he added, "she was obviously from a sheltered home and Japanese ladies know precious little about the realities of the outside world. I don't believe you could understand. Why, they don't even go shopping like American women. The shopkeepers bring everything to them. If she hasn't some place to go—well, you can guess what will happen to her. She could never earn her own living any more than a baby."

"It may end with suicide," I suggested.

Kenjirō doubted that. Suicide is an escape often appealed to in Japan, but he thought that if her temperament had been impulsively capable of seeking such release, she would have made the attempt immediately.

"But," I objected, "isn't your other alternative impossible? Isn't there a rigid law that no woman of the *samurai* class can enter the Yoshiwara?"

"Oh, yes," he said, "but an agent can easily arrange to have her adopted into some family of a lower order and then she loses her rank and its protection."

Alfred came up from his bath and asked us what we were talking about. He had slept through the night.

Antiques, Temples, and Teaching Charm

For many days we had been passing through villages which yielded no good hunting among the antique and second-hand shops. It should be known that the lure of the curio carries poison. Two friends who have lived blithely in affection, confident that no brutal nor subtle assault could ever avail against the harmony of their intimate understanding, perchance step through the doorway of a shop. Presto! A candlestick, a vase, a box, a tumbledown chair, whatever it may be—the desire for the thing magically energizes perception. We suddenly and clearly perceive that the one-time friend at our side is hung with many false tinkling cymbals. We never break the rules of the game; it is the friend who always errs. Thus I was always learning Alfred's abysmal depths, while he was encountering my superlative virtues of unselfishness. However, as his chief fiendishness was for cloisonné and my interest was in carved iron and bronzes and old Kyoto ware, we were spared from too many overdoses of poison.

The little shops of Kami-Suwa really had curios. There were strange, imaginative odds and ends which had been made to please the whims of the eccentrics of a vanished and now almost un-understandable age. Of such whimsicality were the costumes and the heap of personal adornments which we discovered that had once been fashioned for a famous wrestler of Kami-Suwa. Even his sandals were there. He must have been a giant, truly, if his feet filled those *geta*. Everything for the hero had been made in faithful exaggeration to many times the size of the conventional. His leather tobacco pouch was as big as our rucksacks. Every detail of the decorations of the pouch, such as the *netsuke*, was increased to correct proportion. In the stockings for his feet the threads were as thick as whipcord. The grain of the shark skin binding the handle of his sword had come from some fish of the Brobdingnag world. When fully equipped, that famous man—they spoke of him reverently—must have given the effect that he had been blown into expansion by some marvellous pump.

After we had shaken a dozen or so curio shops through our sieve we wandered off into the rain seeking the village temple in the hills. By festivals and gorgeous pageants the people around the shore of Suwa still celebrate their faith and belief that its towns were built by the gods in the beginning of time. The upkeep of the temples, I suppose, must now come from the worshippers or the state as there are no longer lavish feudal patrons with immense incomes of rice. Nevertheless these temples do not seem to suffer poverty.

We easily found the path. A spring bursts from the rock of the precipitous hill behind the temple garden and its waters keep green the shrubs and grasses and the bamboo, and cherish the flowers. Perhaps the garden has achieved its perfection by minute alterations through hundreds of years, but its appeal bespeaks the original conception of its first master artist, who, by creating a subtle absence of formal arrangement, offered the supreme compliment to the beholder to carry on through his own creative imagination that approach to the ideal perfection which can never be reached.

After a time the rain, which had begun falling in torrents, drove us back from the dream garden to the shelter of the overhanging temple roof. A *fusuma* opened behind us and we turned around to see an old woman kneeling on the matting. She bowed low and then arose to disappear and to return again with tea and rice cakes and fruit. She placed the dishes on a low, black lacquer table. We untied our muddy shoes and moved in onto the mats. The rain fell in dull, droning monotony on the tiles of the roof far above our heads. Back in the deep shadows our eyes could see the gleaming of the reddish gold edges of the lacquered idols. Every suggestion was hypnotic of sleep and I had been awake almost all the night before. I grew so sleepy that even the touch of the cup in my hand had the feeling of unreal reality. Between the raising of the cup to my lips and the putting of it down I actually plunged for an instant into sleep, then came to consciousness with a start. I looked at Kenjirō. His eyes were blinking waveringly and with much uncertainty. Were there ever such guests of a temple? I vaguely remember that our hostess put a cushion under my head, and then came a rhythmic coolness from her fan over my face. I would have slept on the rack.

We slept until we awoke to find the sun shining. Our hostess, with immobile, gentle face, was still fanning us. We were abjectly, guiltily remorseful. We sat up and she brought fresh tea. We appealed in a roundabout way for forgiveness by praising the teacups and the teapot. They were very fine. She explained that they had been the gift of some *daimyō*, she thought. Whoever he was, he had made many rich gifts to the temple. She pushed back panels and brought out bowls and vases, and told us romantic legends. The legends were colorful rather than of plot. I knew then that I could never remember more than their impression. The old woman's own personality had drifted into limbo and she had absorbed in its place a reflection of those dark, mysterious temple rooms. She held out robes and porcelains before us and then carried them away quickly. She led us through the shadows, stopping to light incense at the feet of the Buddhas with the reverence that such acts were her life and not her task.

We said goodbye and walked away, following along the crest of the hill. The temple roof disappeared behind the treetops and we were again in the modern world, for at that instant across the valley we saw a huge, nondescript, barracks-like building. It had been erected in the worship of efficiency, and was more completely mere walls of windows with a roof above than even an American factory. As we stood watching, a man paced out of the gate and behind him stepped a girl, and then another girl, and another, until it was a long procession. The line pursued a twisting way, sometimes in measured steps, sometimes in undulating running. At last the line formed a serpentine coil in an open space.

The building was the high school for girls and the man leading the line was the physical instructor. The pupils wore the distinguishing universal reddish-purple skirt of the high schools which are bound over the *yukata*. These skirts look heavy and uncomfortable. They must have been designed by some minister of education in those days of translation when the demand for modern ideas included always that they must be served raw. It was believed with loyalty and devotion that the principle at the base of the secret of foreign success was the axiom that nothing useful can be ornamental.

The physical instructor was inhumanly military and dignified—and so overwhelmingly efficient in his instruction that it was annoying to see such perfection. Secretly perhaps, but always, the male animal instinctively protests and resists that women should unite into solidarity to do things. To his roots he begs that if they do so do, they shall not achieve success in doing so. Man has always run in packs, but woman has been the eternal individual. Our wrath was against the traitor in sleeveless gymnasium shirt and tight foreign trousers who was teaching so systematically and effectively to that line of girls the secret of team work. By the sorrow of his eyes it could be seen he acknowledged to himself his infamy to his sex, but his loyalty to his emperor was that he must conduct that exercise drill and conduct it professionally.

Kenjirō suggested that we visit the school, insisting that such a visit would be considered a great compliment. It seemed to us more like an impertinence of vagrants, but Kenjirō continued firm that it was our duty as itinerant foreigners to interrupt the machinery. He took a couple of our visiting cards, mere innocent slips of pasteboard, and proceeded with his fountain pen to make them pretentiously formidable. He raked up all the detritus of our past lives. We did have sufficiency of conventional shame to cough apologetically when Kenjirō read aloud the outrageous qualifications of our scholarship and degrees which he had added after our names. We learned that it is a mistake to believe that there can be no utilitarian value in a college degree: letters after one's name are seeds ready to burst into useful bloom under an exotic sun, and the flowering may be a pass into a provincial high school for Japanese maidens.

A servant took those remarkable cards from Kenjirō's hand and walked off down the long corridor. The result was that a smiling diplomat came to us empowered to minister to our entertainment and instruction. We were honored as the first courtesy by *not* being allowed to remove our heavy walking shoes. Every step that I took on those shining, spotless floors made me feel as if I were perpetrating a clownish indecency. The remorse that follows one's own wilfulness can never be so keen as the agony when sheer fate ordains unavoidable vulgarity. Still, in leaving heel marks in the polished wood, there was the saving humor of the idea that our hosts thought they were honoring us by encouraging our foreign barbarity.

There were unending rooms of maids in purple skirts. They were studying every sort of subject from the abstract to the practical, and from the aesthetic to the ethical. There were girls with the refinement of profile which one seeks and finds in the ideal drawings by the great Japanese artists. And there were those other faces, the round, good-natured Martha-*sans*. We looked over their shoulders at their paintings of flowers, at their embroidery, at their arithmetic sums, their maps, and their English composition. The Japanese say, "Perhaps rich nations can afford to economize in education and to exploit ignorance, but we, being very poor, must be practical. We cannot take such risk of ignorance."

A modicum of truth lies in the statement that the Japanese have taken up education as a new religion. (And some of the bumptious youthful devotees in Tokyo impress one that it was a mistaken bargain to have allowed them to exchange pocket shrines for text-books.) Theories of education have many splits everywhere in the world and the Japanese fervour has not escaped having to face the necessity of certain decisions. One difference of opinion, which might almost be called theological, rests in the question whether the youth should be educated to think according to conviction or to think according to conformity: to think or to be taught what to think. A Japanese told us that the government must risk its last penny today to guarantee the future, that the people are being educated to understand national policies in the faith that understanding will breed willing cooperation and willing self-sacrifice. When I asked him which he meant, whether students were being taught to understand the policies of the state or whether they were being taught to believe in them, I rather thought that he considered my question argumentative and perhaps unfriendly. However, without his having answered the question, it is obvious that Japan is trusting its fate to the system of educating toward solidarity, the impulse to think alike.

After our noisy boots had been in and out of many rooms we were taken to meet the head of the school. He was not in his administration room, but he entered in a few minutes. After the formal introduction he clapped his hands for tea. His appearance and his dignity were of ancient Japan. His thin divided moustache fell in long pencil-like strands from the corners of his lip, as do those of the sages in the ancient Chinese paintings. His *kimono* was silk. We smoked and drank tea and talked abstractedly about education. It was a girls' school but he talked of boys. We strayed from Montessori methods to industrial training. After he had used some such phrases as "a sound education," Alfred asked how many years of a boy's life he considered should be given over to his schooling. His eyes had been of passive light. They now gleamed like those of a warrior.

"Until he has been taught loyalty to his Emperor!"

It perhaps may be a debatable question for the other nations of the world, that question of Socrates whether virtue can be taught, but the headmaster of the high school in Kami-Suwa declared that in Japan a teacher is not a teacher unless he can teach loyalty. The boys must be taught loyalty; the daughters of the empire must be taught grace. (And by grace I think he meant also charm.) To exemplify, we were led to the "flower-arranging room." The Japanese arranging of flowers is a ceremony and there is commingled in it both the suggestion of the actual in life and the ideal of the perfect. The room which we were shown was an attempt to achieve the supreme inheritance of Japanese art in architecture and decoration— rhythm, harmony, and simplicity. Something of the spirit of didacticism must ever hang over a room so built but, in the room that we were shown, charm and beauty had surprisingly survived the inevitable refrigeration of being labelled "classic."

Tsuromatsu and Hisumatsu

In the same town of Kami-Suwa where the barracks-like high school for girls spreads its wings there also rises the tiled roof of a *geisha* house. Under its protection other daughters of the Empire are also being rigorously trained to duties—the life of amusing and entertaining. The position of the *geisha* cannot be illuminated by comparisons. There are the "sing-song girls" of Beijing and the nautch dancers of India, and there were in the days of the fruition of Greek civilization the sisters of Aspasia. The life of the *geisha* might be considered to be somewhat parallel to their lives in so far as it is a response to the demand of highly civilized man for the romance of idealized anarchy, the inhibitions of custom, or dogma, having precluded the expression of inborn romantic desire in his conventional life. Men whose minds have realized some measure of freedom through imagination and culture instinctively seek idealistic companionship with women. When its realization is compressed by such custom as marriage by family arrangement this desire finds expression in some direction where there is at least the illusion of freedom. Human nature is like the human body, if pressure is applied in one spot, unless there is some equitable, compensating bulge elsewhere, the compression is likely to be vitally destructive. If the highest ideality has as its cornerstone responsibility, then when marriage is an institution by arrangement and the sense of responsibility is not created through the freedom of choice, feminine companionship and charm will inevitably be sought in the romance of some more voluntary arrangement. Who will absolutely deny that when the endeavour to save poetical yearning from defeat in such companionship as the almost classical ceremony of watching the white fingers of a *geisha* pour tea into a shell of porcelain, a sort of mutual sense of responsibility to save the fineness of life may enter into the relationship as a redeeming grace against the professionalism of the *geisha's* life?

We turned from the street into the gate of the principal tea-house. There was a clapping of hands by the first servant who heard our steps on the gravel path and in a moment the mistress and all the men-servants and maid-servants were at the door to greet us. It was at an hour in the afternoon when the tea-house did not expect guests. We took off our shoes and were led to the floor above. There were four or five rooms but they soon became one, the maids removing the *fusuma*, and we were given the luxury of unpartitioned possession. One side, entirely without wall, overhung the garden.

The maids brought cold water and tea and sherbets and iced beer and fruits and cakes, and there were dishes on the table of which we did not even lift the covers. Then they knelt and awaited our orders whether they should send for *geisha*. They explained that at that hour there might be the rude annoyance to our honorable patience of having to endure an unavoidable delay. It would not be likely that the *geisha* could come immediately. We told them that our honorable patience would suffer the delay.

When the French builders and decorators tried to attain the ultimate for the housing of royalty in the age of the Grand Monarch, their success approached close to the realization of what the imagination of the period asked. Versailles was built with the idea of reaching theoretical perfection through the completion of detail. The imagination of the beholder was supposed to find complete satisfaction in what he saw and not to feel the urge of the possibility of still higher flights. If the beholder was not content with this "perfection," he was indeed in a plight, for there was no next step except to begin all over again. The rhythm of the art of the Japanese tea-house is not dependent upon regularity nor balance. Its perfection can never be completed. The last word cannot be spoken. It is like life.

We walked over the soft mats examining the work of the craftsman builder who had made his material yield its beauty through the grain and line of each plank, board, beam, pillar, and panel. I moved a cushion to the balcony and sat down to study the room in deeper perspective. I never followed out this sedate contemplation, for instead I happened to look over the balcony. Across the court of the garden I saw into an open room of a wing. Three little girls, from about five to seven years of age, were being trained in the arts of the *geisha*. At that moment their instruction was in the dance.

The work was being gone through seriously but the teachers were sympathetic and encouraging. A dancing master assumed the general superintendence: several older girls, full-fledged *geisha*, sat offering suggestions from their experience. They were in simple, everyday dress and not in *geisha* costume. The novitiates sometimes begin their training even younger than five years. Quite often such children are orphans who come into the profession by legal adoption. Others are the children of parents who have apprenticed their daughters under an arrangement which virtually amounts to a sale. Naturally the *geisha* master does not select children who do not possess the promise of grace, beauty, and charm. The long training is expensive and it is intended that there shall be a return on the investment. The little girls, whom we could see, were practising over and over again the steps of some classical dance to the music of a *shamisen*. From the expression of their faces to the position of their fingers in carrying their fans, every possibility of technique which should enter into the dance was receiving the minutest attention.

For many years, Kenjirō whispered, the training of those little girls must go on to one end—to interest, to entertain, and to amuse men. They will be taught to wear the gorgeous silks and embroideries of the *geisha*. They will be taught that every movement of the hand and arm in pouring tea or passing the cup should be an art. They will be taught when they should smile, when they should laugh, and when they should sympathize. They will be taught how to converse, how to repeat the classical tales and the tales of folklore and how deftly to introduce merry stories of the day. After all this training the graduation comes when they enter actively into the life of the *geisha*. In this budding a girl may amuse partly by the mere gossamer fragility of her youth, but later maturity brings the capital of acquired experience, not only in the art of entertaining but through having learned that the charm of woman is largely the solace that she can bring through sympathy and understanding.

What is the end? It may be better or worse, tragic or domestic, marriage, shame, servitude, modest anonymity, or the retirement to the teaching of her art to another generation. Her life is one obviously wherein the path has many by-ways to temptation. There is much that must be insincere and tinsel. If many a little heart, sweet, modest, and unhardened, is crushed, nevertheless if there be forgiving gods among those to whom she prays, surely those gods must know that these Mary Magdalenes are (so a poet of the Yoshiwara wrote) in the greater truth as the flowers of the lotus. Though their feet have touched the black mud of the stagnant pond, "the heart of the *geisha* is the flower of the lotus."

We heard a footstep at the door and turned to see a *geisha* standing there. She was tall and slender. The delicate paleness of her face was even whiter through fear. She saw us, barbarians, sitting in the refinement of the tea-house room. The carmine spots on her lips shone brightly, giving to her expression the unreality of the frightened look a doll might have if suddenly brought to life. She was carrying a *shamisen*. Her fingers tightly clutched the wrappings. She came across the room toward us and as her knees bent against the skirt of her *kimono* I could see that they were trembling. She sat down and tried to smile. The duty of a *geisha* is to smile. She smiled with the same last effort of loyalty which carries the soldier into a hopeless charge.

I felt an abysmal brute to be there. Absurd perhaps, but it was as if the command of some strange, scornful, hitherto unheeded, almost unknown spirit of justice was calling me to name some defense why man in his arrogance has assumed the right to pluck the beauty of the flowers and has assumed the justification that the reason for the perfume and the beauty is that they were created for him. It was a strange beginning for the gaiety of a *geisha* luncheon.

Tsuromatsu drew back the fold of her sleeve to her elbow and raised the teapot. The spout trembled against the rim of the cup which she was filling. She handed the cup to Kenjirō and until that moment I do not believe that she had noticed that he was a Japanese.

"The child is frightened to death," said Alfred. "Say something, Kenjirō, quick! If she wants to go home——"

Tsuromatsu had read the meaning of the words from their tone before Kenjirō tried to translate. She smiled and this time her lips parted from her pretty teeth spontaneously. Then she said that Hisumatsu, a second *geisha*, would soon come. When the messenger had arrived for them they had first to send for their hair dresser. The messenger had told them that the guests at the tea-house were foreigners. Thus her frightened anticipation had had its beginning before she had entered the room. We asked what had been her fears.

Tsuromatsu did not wish to say. She had once before seen foreigners but only from her balcony. We still persisted in our question. When she realized that the truth would please us more than compliments, even if the telling somewhat offended against the etiquette of hospitality, she ventured slowly to repeat some of the tales which had been passed along by imaginative tongues until they had eventually reached the *geisha* house of Kami-Suwa. We sat waiting to hear some legend truly scandalous, but there was nothing of such atrocity. She had not heard of Buddhist children being stolen for sacrifice on Christian altars. Our barbarities of the Western world that worried the *geisha* sensibility were departures not from mercy but from manners. We were wild and rough and very noisy, always in a hurry, knowing nothing of the refinements, such as tea drinking, and we were always dropping rice grains from our chopsticks onto the floor. And, as a conclusion, the foreigner, such was her information, had no appreciation for gentle conversation, nor for any of the arts of social intercourse of which the *geisha*, in her vocation, is the guardian priestess.

Of all the intricacies of thought in modern Japan, the most interesting is the side-by-side existence (without its possession seemingly arousing any astonishment in the mind of the possessors) of two completely different conceptions of the foreigner. A Japanese may sometimes sincerely render honor to a foreigner for superior attainments and yet sustain the old feudal idea that the foreigner must be a barbarian even in those very attainments. It is quite possible when the frightened Tsuromatsu left the *geisha* house in her *rikisha* that she not only felt that she was going to an ordeal where she would suffer from the crudities of the *inferior* foreigner, but that she was being singled out for the distinct honor of entertaining the *superior* foreigner. In one way, for the common people, this paradox may be partially explained by the fact that their leaders order them to honor the foreigner for his practical achievements, and in their unhesitating loyalty they do as they are told. It is much easier to accept such authority than to puzzle out how the knowledge and experience of their worshipped ancestors could have been of such superior brand and yet been of such ignorance.

Tsuromatsu was telling us something of her fears when Hisumatsu entered. Upon what scene she had expected to come, I have no imagining, but her surprise at the state of intimate peace which did reign proved that she had been thinking of a different probability. Her surprise dissipated her timidity, and she began to laugh at Tsuromatsu's earnestness. Hisumatsu was somewhat older. Her *geisha* dress was perhaps richer. Quite likely her skill in conversation and in playing the *shamisen* was superior—but she was not so exquisitely fragile in her beauty.

Japan is the court of Harun al-Raschid in the love of hearing stories. Always we were being asked for stories, stories of romance, love, and adventure, "such as you tell at home when sitting on the mats drinking tea." Perhaps the elevation to chairs has subtly sapped away from us the art of tale spinning beyond the briefest of anecdotes and jokes. There was no more of a response in us when Tsuromatsu asked us to tell a story than there had been when Kenjirō had asked us to extemporize poetry in the valley of the Kiso River. We scored a failure as always but a moment later chance gave us a second opportunity for the vindication of Occidental accomplishments.

Alfred had picked up a *shamisen* and was searching for some harmonics in the long strings. In the mystery of the night, coming out of the darkness, the music of Japan has a certain functioning charm harmonizing with the rhythm of the wings of insects beating their way through the shadows. But to hear the love song of a strident cicada coming from the white throat and red lips of a *geisha*—at least that is not our melody of passion. It was Hisumatsu this time who made the request. She asked Alfred to sing a song, "as you sing songs in America." This was the chance to redeem our failure. The hills of Norway gave Alfred a birth-gift of melody. His whistling is like a bird call, clear and true. Kenjirō and I insisted that he must whistle. It was the air of a folksong that he remembered. It had the Viking cry of the Norse wind and the lust of storm and battle. The two girls tried to listen.

"Change to *Pagliacci*," I whispered. The music of the North had failed. I was in duress to save our faces.

Again they tried to listen. Then they looked at each other in astonishment and in each pair of eyes there was annoyance. They began talking to each other in disregard of *Pagliacci* and everything Italian. It was an obvious disregard. At first they had thought that he might be practising, but when he continued the distressing sounds, then they were sure that we were making fun of their request. They were trying to save their own faces. They had begun talking to prove that they could not so easily be taken in. Kenjirō had the brilliancy to retreat. He hastened to ask them to sing and play again. By sitting raptly while the strings of the *shamisen* were rasped by the sharp ivory pick and their voices followed in accompaniment, we were able in a measure to atone for the barbarity of our own music by showing that we could listen appreciatively to good music when opportunity granted.

The hour came to pay our reckoning and to depart. We said goodbye over the teacups, but when we were sitting at the door putting on our shoes we heard the sound of the *geisha*' white *tabi* on the stairs. Their two *rikisha* wheeled up to the entrance for them, but they hesitated. They stood whispering to each other for a moment and then turned to us and suggested that they would walk as far as our inn gate with us if we wished. Alfred and I were nonplussed. Kenjirō hurriedly told us that their suggestion was a marked compliment, that we should accept it with thanks, and that he would explain later. Sometimes—and the occasions are supposed to be so sufficiently rare as to be of complimentary value—a popular *geisha* will drag the hem of her embroidered *kimono* along the street in this custom of courtesy by which she shows her appreciation for her entertainment. It should be remembered that a *geisha* is traditionally a guest. In Tokyo, said Kenjirō, a young blood who has spent his last spendthrift *sen* on a gorgeous dinner will await such approval as the hallmark upon his artistry as host. If it is denied he reads in the answer not a mere feminine caprice but an impartial, critical disapproval. He seeks for the reason by trying to remember any errors in his own hostly proficiency. It is to be imagined, however, that while the bestowal of this approval may theoretically only be employed for the maintenance of the rigid standard of etiquette and artistry, in practice it is not always confined to such rarefied judgment.

The five of us started on the long walk to the inn gate. I am afraid that the gentle *geisha* had not given thought to the composition of the picture. Tsuromatsu was rather tall for a Japanese, but Hisumatsu was not, and the *seiyō-jin* were somewhat over six feet each. In the daylight, also, the *geisha* costume noticeably brightens a street. Walking abreast we made a cordon stretching across the road to the utter bewilderment of Kami-Suwa.

We had found before this that the crowds which gather in provincial towns are seldom intentionally annoying, although sometimes they do jam around a shop door, shutting off the light and air. The steadfast staring may be unpleasant, but the foreigner soon learns to think little about naive curiosity. Our march through Kami-Suwa certainly did attract attention, but the crowds separated and allowed us to pass without following at our heels, and I believed Kenjirō when he said that this heroic restraint of curiosity arose from their innate feeling that its manifestation would be discourteous and inhospitable. This sense of consideration was not a sufficiently quick reaction, however, to prevent inordinate amazement when anyone met us suddenly. A boy on a bicycle, coming round a corner, forgot his own personal existence entirely and his unguided wheel carried him directly into a shop door, somewhat to the disturbance of the ménage and himself. Our progress continued slowly as the toed-in sandals under the long *kimono* skirts of the *geisha* did not take steps measuring with our usual stride. We found that dictionary conversation could not be pursued expeditiously in the street, and after a few attempts to make known words do the work of unknown with discouraging results, the advance proceeded silently and rather solemnly, although I received flashes from those two demure maids that they had a sense of humor. The corners of their mouths did twitch in mischievous enjoyment of the situation.

When we reached the shores of the lake we sat down on the rocks and watched the boats. The rising breeze roughened the surface into a long path of flame against the red sun. Hisumatsu had been dissatisfied all afternoon with the hurried effort of her hairdresser. She drew out the large combs and the heavy strands of hair fell over her shoulders. She told us a queer, whimsical story about the birds that were flying over the reeds. They said goodbye to us and walked away and we turned in at our inn lane.

Our dinner was very late. Finally the stumbling maid came, rubbing her eyes and yawning. She was, as always we had seen her, on the immediate point of going to sleep. She had been carrying *sake*, all the night before, but she had been almost as sleepy on the previous day. Now, in serving dinner, she went definitely to sleep every time there was a lull in her duties. She had one hiatus of lukewarm wakefulness in which she mumbled some appeal to Kenjirō, but he declared to us that the words had no sense. We began fearing for the few faculties she appeared to have.

Kenjirō listened more carefully. "I believe she is saying something," he decided.

Little by little we learned that she had a favor to ask the foreign doctor. Just how she had discovered that Alfred had medical wisdom was a mystery. She said that all Japan knows that foreign doctors can do anything. She begged for a drug to keep her awake, something that she could swallow so that she would never feel sleepy again, or better than that, some drug so potent, if there were any such, that she would never even have to sleep again.

"H'm," said the foreign doctor. "Tell her there isn't any such drug. Tell her to get a good night's sleep. She will feel better about it in the morning."

Her disappointment was pitiful.

"But I shall never have a night's sleep," she said. "If I ask for time to sleep I shall be told that there are many maids who will be glad to take my place." She knew, she went on, that she was very stupid, but she maintained that she was not so stupid when she was not so sleepy.

It is outside our comprehension and experience how the Chinese and Japanese can labour on and on, more nearly attaining a wakeful condition for the full round of the day than the individuals of other races would consent to endure even if they could continue life under the strain. In all inns the maids work long hours, nor do the mistresses spare themselves. The mistress of the inn at Kami-Suwa seemingly lacked the usual kindly sympathy for her maids and was unusually demanding. Hana-*san* (the irony of calling her a *flower*!) could not dare the risk of attempting to escape from her slavery. It was for the sake of her fatherless child that she dared not, she told us. She, the clumsy, stumbling, stupid, sleepy maid, had had her tragedy as had had the pale, forsaken daughter of the nobility whom she had waited upon the night before.

After her disappointment that she could obtain from us no sleep-dispelling drug she toppled again into unconsciousness. We could at least give her temporary help. We sent for the mistress and asked her for a full night's sleep for the girl. For the maid's sake it was necessary to put our demand on the ground that we must have better service in the morning. This saved the face of the mistress. After the mistress had consented and had gone, poor Hana-*san*'s affectionate thanks were embarrassing.

On a point reaching into the lake and under our balcony stood a small, one-storied shrine. It was sheltered by a tiled roof pitched on four columns. We saw from our room two figures in white walking along the shore. They stopped at the shrine and knelt for some time. When they arose the bright moon suddenly revealed that the two figures were Tsuromatsu and Hisumatsu. Kenjirō went down to speak to them and in a moment their three heads appeared up the stairs. The *geisha* had changed the silks and brocades of their costume for simple white *yukata* and their hair was not now arranged after the elaborate style of the professional hairdresser. Instead of this simplicity detracting it quite startlingly bespoke the charm of their delicate beauty.

They were embarrassed and they were blushing. It was one thing to have it their duty to be whirled in *rikisha* to a tea-house to meet strange patrons, but to pay an informal visit at our rooms, especially at that hour, was quite another affair, and most unconventional. They were shocked at their own impulsiveness in having run up the stairs and they were very much afraid that someone in the inn would discover their presence. The little shrine, it appeared, was in especial favor with the members of the *geisha* house where they lived, and they often came, particularly if the moon were shining in the early evening, to worship before their duties called. We opened our rucksacks and found some odds and ends which we made do for presents. They chatted for a moment and then ran off into the night.

Later Kenjirō told me that as they were going they had asked us to be their guests at the theatre—there was a performance of one of the classic dramas by a travelling troupe from Tokyo—and afterwards to have supper at the tea-house.

Kenjirō's explanation of his refusal was rather intricate and elaborate, but stripped of *bushidō* I think the inner simplicity was that he had suffered enough for one day from the conspicuous exhibition of our long legs and he had no desire for being responsible for taking them into a crowded Japanese theatre.

A Log of Incidents

It was dark and threatening the next morning but we decided to be on our way. We bought a couple of paper umbrellas. We soon found that when we needed them at all that day we needed a roof much more. Kenjirō was off on his bicycle and we arranged to overtake him at the village of Fujimi. We were hardly out of Kami-Suwa before we had to make our first dash for shelter to escape drowning in the open road. The thatched house which we besieged for shelter would probably have been most picturesque on a sunny day but it was exceedingly primitive for a storm. Our hostess was a very old woman, diminutive and smiling. The rain pounded against her hut and discovered every possible chance to force its way in. She tried to start a fire from damp sticks and charcoal and succeeded after a long effort. The fire was to heat the water for our tea. It was useless to protest. No guests might leave her house unhonored by a cup of tea.

Japan never seems so remote from the West as when seen through the rain. Fishermen, in straw raincoats, were wading in the creeks with hand nets. The children in the villages were wading in the gutters.

The towns seemed self-sufficient and prosperous. They had captured the mountain streams and had led them away from their channels to run in deep, wide canals through the streets. Innumerable waterwheels drew upon this energy for the miniature factories. We were walking through one of these towns—the sun was shining brightly at the moment—when there was a sprinkling of giant drops. We knew that that meant another cloudburst and we turned in at the first door. It was a barber's shop. We asked permission for standing room, but the men who had been sitting around a large brazier lifted it away and insisted upon giving us their places on the matting.

The chairs, the mirrors, the shampoo bowls, the razors, and all the rest of the elaborate paraphernalia looked so immaculate and usable that I expected Alfred to decide that it would be discourteous for him to waste such an opportunity of having his beard trimmed. He surprised me by suggesting that we toss up to see which one should make the experiment of the complete surrender to all the inventions. Perhaps he was tactfully suggesting that my unkemptness showed the greater necessity, but the turn of the coin made him the adventurer.

The rain was now falling so that it swept the streets in a flood. The thunder was shaking the hills. A thunderstorm, for me, is the most soporific inducer in the world and my eyes began to waver and soon I was many times asleep. When I awoke, under Alfred's urge, the sun was out again. My joints were stiff, I was sleepy, and I was old, but the world seemed very new after its scrubbing, and nothing less than jauntiness could express the state of transformation, brought about by clippers, shears, hot towels, and everything that went with the treatment, in the appearance of my companion. The barber and his two assistants, with their huge palm fans, were bowing and smiling with an air of complete satisfaction. I was out of sympathy both with refurnished nature and the revamped man. I remarked irritably that his pursuit of beauty would be the ruination of our joint purse.

"Yes," he said, "and the fees equalled the bill. I had to pay some rent for your taking up the entire floor for your siesta."

The bill had been five *sen* and the fees had been five *sen*, so that altogether we had squandered five cents of our money.

Fujimi is little more than a hamlet. It is tucked away in a fold of the hills off the main paths of the trail. Its days are probably as ancient as the worship of Fuji-*san*. The view of the sacred mountain from Fujimi is a paradox of the beautiful. The sudden sight of the blue outline of the mountain against the sky comes crushingly into one's consciousness as an extraordinary awakening and quickening, and yet the emotion is deep, reverent, and silent. Maybe it was our undue imagination but the peasants of the valley seemed marked by quietude. While Fuji-*san* was cloud hidden that first day, on the long walk of the next we found the lonely laborers of the isolated farm terraces often staying their work for a moment, their consciousness lost in passionate gaze toward the sacred slope.

It was only by much questioning of the peasants whom we met on the road that we were able to find the hamlet. Once when we were unable to understand the answer, with a quick smile to disarm our protests, the questioned one turned back his steps until he could point out the path. We had been swinging along at our best pace in the hours between torrents and it was not long after midday when we found Kenjirō's bicycle outside an inn. Alfred declared that our sixteen or so miles had not aroused him from the sluggishness brought on by a full day's rest at Kami-Suwa and he was for going on, but as the rain was now falling again, this time in a settled drizzle, he had to be a martyr to enduring a roof over his head or else to seek his own drenching.

The inn was the most meagre in ordinary equipment of any that we had found. It was not much more than a rest-house, although it had evidently at one time been of more pretense. The fear expressed by our host that his house was unworthy had the ardour of conviction. In order to know better what to borrow from his neighbors for the entertainment of the *seiyō-jin* he suggested a scale of three prices. We chose the middle quotation of one *yen*, twenty *sen* (sixty cents). The fire was then started in the kitchen.

Japanese architecture is said to be in direct line of descent from the nomadic tent of Central Asia. Just as the roof and the four corner posts are the essentials of the tent, in the building of a Japanese house, the corner posts are first set up and the roof is built next. Our inn might have served this theory of descent as an admirable example. The roof was the chief reason for its existence. There were no wings. The stairway was on the outside, coming up through the balconies which ran completely around the two upper floors. In winter days when wooden shutters enclose and darken the rooms the bare simplicity may grow dreary. The wind is then the father of shivering drafts which creep over the floor, but for the days of summer, when the green valley of Fujimi lies in the shelter of the great granite ranges, the memory of the stifling cave-like rooms of our Western architecture seemed barbarous and of dull imagination in comparison. The philosophy of Japan's housebuilding appears to be that it is better fully to live with nature in nature's season of wakefulness than to invent a compromise shelter equally reserved against nature through the revolution of the year.

Alfred had gone exploring to find the bath. A few minutes later our host excitedly came up the stairs to warn us that the bearded foreigner was tempting destruction. Rumor that foreigners have experimented with cold baths and have discovered reactions within themselves to endure such rigor had not reached Fujimi. When the impatient foreigner had learned that the hot bath was not ready, he filled the tub with the icy water that came spouting through a bamboo pipe. In the midst of our efforts to calm our host, Alfred himself appeared, red and beaming. Nevertheless, neither his rosiness nor his exhilaration could allure Kenjirō and me into following his recommendation to go and do likewise. We decided, instead, to take the host's advice. He sent us to the public baths. Armed with towels, and in borrowed *yukata* and borrowed wooden *geta*, we set forth. My *yukata* came to my knees, no lower, and it was restricted in other dimensions. For the women and children sitting in the doorways our progress through the street may have brought some interest into a rainy and perhaps otherwise dull afternoon.

The baths, housed in a low, small, ramshackle building, were famous for leagues about. The keeper of the baths was a "herbist." He went out into the mountains—on stealthy and secret excursions which the cleverest tracker had never followed—and brought back sweet-scented hay which his wife sewed into bags and threw into the hot water. Everything about the discovery, she said, was their own secret. Whatever was the secret of the herbs, the natural, delicate perfume was pleasing. The two tubs for the men were fairly large tanks. They had been freshly filled with heated spring water just before we entered. It was not yet the men's hour, but a half-dozen women were in their half of the building, either busily pouring water over themselves on the scrubbing platform or sitting placidly up to their chins in the hot water. The mistress was most energetic. She had a pair of large scrubbing brushes which she was applying to their backs. Back scrubbing in Japan is an ancient institution and the practice may have some real physiological merit. At least the vigorous scrubbing up and down the vertebrae produces a soothing and restful reaction.

A phrase that I had come across in my dictionary had stuck in my memory. Translated, it was: "Will you kindly honor me by scrubbing my back?" I asked Kenjirō whether my remembrance and pronunciation of the Japanese words were correct.

"Pretty good," he said, and then I saw a slumbering twinkle in his black eyes. "But why do you practise on me? Why don't you say it to the mistress to see whether she will understand?"

"Stop!" I spluttered. But it was too late. He had called out to the busy mistress to ask the foreigner to ask to have his back scrubbed. Until that moment we had been inconspicuous in our dark end of the room, but now everybody looked up and edged along for the entertainment of hearing a foreigner speak Japanese. I was responding, but my phrases were directed at Kenjirō and had nothing to do with back scrubbing.

There are exigencies of fate which come down upon one like an avalanche. The revenue to the busy mistress from the use of her scrubbing brush was three *sen* from each person, which was a full *sen* more than for the bath itself, and thus business was business and a serious matter with her. She descended upon me with her three-legged stool and scrubbing brushes and proceeded to earn the extra *sen*. I was completely cowed by her determination.

We sat parboiling ourselves in the tub for some time. All the customers had now either been scrubbed or had not asked to be scrubbed, and the mistress could sit down for a moment to rest and to talk. Particularly did she talk. She talked on and on, exploiting the merits of the local advantages of Fujimi. Ah, where could one go to find Fujimi's equal? Such views! And we must promise to visit the tea-house. It was unfair to refuse that to Fujimi. The maids, it was true, were not *geisha*, but they were every bit as talented as any *geisha* of Tokyo, and sang and played and danced far better than provincial *geisha*.

Back in our inn the extra twenty *sen* apiece above the minimum rate had wrought marvels in the kitchen. We were hungry. We were always hungry. And we had learned always to expect the inn dinners to satisfy our demands. That night we truly had marvellous dishes. The bamboo shoots were as tender as bamboo shoots can be. Whether supreme genius or chance was responsible for the sauce for the chicken, the result was perfection. Dinner was very early. After the meal I found a longer *yukata* and, as the rain had stopped for an interval, Kenjirō and I walked to a hill to see the sunset. On our way back we passed the tea-house which had been so enthusiastically recommended by the mistress of the baths. We went in. Green peaches were brought to us to nibble at, and tea and warm beer to sip.

The house was indeed gorgeous with its gold *fusuma* and polished wood. The decorations almost kept within traditional taste, and simplicity had not been too grievously erred against. But the atmosphere of proportion and rhythm had been missed by that narrow margin which perversely is more irritating inversely to the width of the escape. We may possibly have had the added impulse to this critical judgment by the insidious predilection of the mosquitoes for us rather than for the two maids who were paring the peaches. One of them explained that the mosquitoes of Fujimi are famous for preferring outsiders.

Two of the rooms were crowded with supper parties, of wine, women, and song, but compared to the revelries of bucolic bloods in other lands, something might be said in praise of such restraint as prevailed in the Fujimi tea-house. It may be no honor nor compliment to the spirit of refinement to wish vice as well as virtue clothed in some modicum of grace and retirement, but it does make the world easier to live in.

The soft rain stopped dripping from the eaves some time in the night and the sky was clear when the sun leaped above the mountain ridge, as if impatient to find the radiance of the glorious, virginal day. The green of the valley was a glowing emerald and the mountains were sharp and grey with no shielding haze.

Our host sent his daughter to lead us through a shortcut in the hills to the main road. Kenjirō, with his bicycle, had to take the conventional path. The little *musume* trotted along at our side with a full sense of responsibility, her feet twinkling down the rocky pitches, her *yukata* sleeves fluttering out like wings. Suddenly she pointed the way and then, before we could thank her, ran back. Skipping and dancing she ran, reaching out her hands to the leaves on the bushes or waving them to the flying insects.

The rain clouds had hidden Fuji-*san* the day before. On this morning as we came through the sharp cut in the rocks which led to the main road, outlined against the sky we saw the long purple slope. We climbed to a terrace on the side of a granite block and sat with our feet dangling and our chins in our hands. There was one white cloud, no bigger than a man's hand. It floated slowly toward the crater and then hesitated above the snow ribs on the sides. Then came another cloud across the sky, then another and another, until the summit was hidden by the glowing veils. We slid down from our rock and walked on toward the mountain.

From the day that we left the plains and turned into the hills our tramping had been long climbs but now the road again dropped away toward the lowlands. We had easily forgotten the hours of dancing heat waves, but, with a start, I began to remember Nagoya, of the rice plains, of those stifling nights and brazen days. The memory had also grown dim of my once rhapsodical joy in finding shaved ice to slake my dusty thirst. If I had never known anything but the quiet, velvet smoothness of water from wells and springs and the knowledge of the grind of ice particles against my tongue had been denied me, then I might well have mistaken affection for passion. There was no spring nor stream to be found. The lower path of the widening valley was growing into a road but we were following a trail higher up on the ridge. Down under the leaves of the trees we thought we saw a thatched roof. If there was a house there, there would be water. We found a path downward by making it, and we were rewarded by seeing a house under the trees.

An old woman was reeling silk from the cocoons which she had floating in a bowl of hot water. She glanced up casually when she heard our step, but when she saw what she saw her mouth and eyes opened and the cocoons dropped from her fingers. It was the purity of absolute surprise without admixed fear or any other diluting emotion. I began to doubt that she would ever have another emotion but at last the need for breath racked her, and the resulting gasp freed her from the spell of silence which, indeed, was a most unusual state. She assailed us with a deluge of questions. With every possible variation of the query she demanded to know if we were really foreigners. I was repeating, "*Hai, hai, seiyō-jin*" as best I could when I heard coming through the valley the welcome rattle of the demon bicycle.

I turned over my task to Kenjirō and he took up the assurance to the old woman that she was actually in the presence of flesh and blood foreigners. With his every reiteration the wider became the smile of her satisfaction. She stood on one foot and then the other and clapped her hands and finally ran across the road to another house. She called into the door and a young woman came out. The girl was the wife of her grandson and the explanations had to be made over again for her. Then we sat down on the floor and she brought tea and cold water and red peaches. The questions still came. Our wrinkled hostess was a delighted child. She stared at one of us and then turned to stare at the other. At last she settled a continuing gaze upon me. She was enduring some restraint but it could be humanly endured no longer. She walked over to me and naively unbuttoned the top buttons of my flannel shirt.

"It is so," she said to her granddaughter-in-law, "they are white all over."

When we got up to go I asked permission to take her picture. We all stepped into the road together. When the camera clicked and was again in my rucksack, she dramatically raised her eyes to the mountain tops and gave us her *vale*.

"I am eighty years old. I have never seen a foreigner. I have wanted all my life to see a foreigner. Now that I have seen foreigners I can die happy."

We gave her one of our paper umbrellas as a remembrance so that if she should wake up the next morning with a doubt that it had all really happened there would be that visible evidence standing in the corner. The testimony of our visitation in the shape of a fifteen-cent umbrella was evidently appreciated. She took it cherishingly in her arms as if it were newborn and of flickering life.

It is fourteen miles by railroad from Fujimi to Hinoharu. The railroad would be the shortest distance for a crow, but even that bird might find himself the blacker if he should essay the long, sooted tunnels. We found many extra miles by exploring the up-and-down paths for the changing views of Fuji-*san*, but nevertheless it was early in the afternoon when we reached Hinoharu. I then discovered two shaved ice shops, one after the other, and the intoxication pitched my mood to full ebulliency. For one day Alfred could have as much walking as he could digest as far as I was concerned. We shouldered our rucksacks and Kenjirō coasted off down the hill with the promise of a welcome of shaved ice and a hot bath at the best inn in Nirasaki.

Some distance out of Hinoharu and well into the country we discovered two brothers of the road. They were trying to manufacture a cup out of a piece of bamboo to reach into the recesses of the rocks to get at the water of a trickling spring. We offered them the aid of our aluminum cup.

Japan may affirm, as she does, the non-existence of any variety of native hobo, but I am sure that either of our new friends would have answered to the call of "Hello, Jack!" After salutations and thanks were passed, Alfred and I climbed up the bank to the plot of grass in front of a wayside temple and sat down for a contemplative rest in the shade. We always tempted calamity, it seemed, when we tried to rest under the shadow of a temple. The two Jacks came tumbling after and shared our cigarettes with Oriental appreciation. They were rather picturesque individuals. Their cotton clothes were not only in tatters but were imaginatively patched. In a land where there is nudity and not nakedness patches do seem an affectation of the imagination.

I was sleepy from the sun and I dropped back in a natural couch between the roots of a tree and pulled my cork helmet down over my face to keep off the flies, leaving to Alfred the study of the habits and customs of the Japanese tramp. As I lay there in drowsy half-sleep one of those companions, so I judged from the sounds which crept under my hat into my ears, was suffering from a mood of restlessness. Also he was afflicted with a strange, gasping wheeze. I had just reached the point of being interested enough to look out from under my hat when a panting breath was expulsed over my neck, and my hat arose from no effort of mine. I was left lying between the roots to look into a pair of pitiless, yellow eyes.

It took me a frigid moment to discover that my vis-à-vis was a horse. The animal stood over me, holding my hat in his teeth just beyond any sudden swing of my hand. After he had had sufficiency of staring he tossed his head, still holding fast to the hat, and ambled off towards the road. I jumped to my feet and followed. As soon as the bony, ill-kempt creature stepped out of the temple grounds his malevolence vanished. He dropped the hat into the gutter and jogged away to find a more conventional pasture. We could now add animals to the list of uncanny powers that from time to time had driven us from resting in temple grounds. I had no temper left for facing the laughter of the two Japanese tramps. I called back to Alfred that I was on my way and he kindly brought my rucksack.

Instead of the usual sharp differentiation between city and country, Nirasaki has an indefinite beginning of straggling houses. The town lies along the shore of the Kamanashi River, which has cut its way through the granite rocks of the valley, a strong current flowing a thick, whitish grey color. As we were entering the outskirts we heard the shrill whistle of the reed pipe of a pedlar and a moment later we saw him coming out of a gate carrying his swinging boxes of trays hung from a yoke across his shoulders. He was so abnormally tall for a Japanese that we quickened our step to have a look at him. He dropped the reed from his lips to sing-song his wares—odds and ends of shining trumpery. The words were Japanese but the intoning called us back to China, and when we saw his face we were sure that he was a Manchu. He knew the last ingratiating artifice that has ever been accredited either to pedlar or Celestial. We delayed to appreciate his technique, to see him approach the women of the open-sided houses, and to fascinate them by the intensity of his will to please, and also by his ingratiating gallantry.

"Take care!" we felt like saying oracularly to all Japan. "Take care that you never attempt the conquest of China. China may be conquered but never the Chinese. They will rise up and slay you not by arms but by serving you better than you can serve yourselves."

We found Kenjirō resting in an ice shop. He had judged truly that the easiest way to find us was to let us find him, trusting that as long as I had a *sen* I would never pass a *kōri* flag. The very pretty maid had her *yukata* sleeves tied back from her graceful arms. I do not know what story Kenjirō had concocted to tell her but after she had handed me my cupful of snow she watched me steadily with the air that she expected black magic at any moment. I caught a glimpse of Kenjirō's twinkle. I was filled with suspicion. Finally the maid turned upon Kenjirō in exasperation and said many things. Some strange tale told about foreigners must have been one of Kenjirō's best creations, but in some way we had failed to live up to our heralding. She was exceedingly pretty and a pretty girl in a pretty tempest is just as interesting and bewitching in Nirasaki as in any other spot in the world. However, any translation of his tale to her Kenjirō refused absolutely.

Jnn Maids and the Elixir of Life

The native inn is such an interweaving of privacy with no privacy at all that if the traveller has a sympathetic liking for the hospitality it should be put down to his temperament rather than to his reasonableness or unreasonableness. Calling upon all his reasonableness, the foreigner may still be miserable amid Japanese customs if he were born to a different crystallization. Kenjirō considered the inn at Nirasaki to be rather superior to the average, meaning, I judged, not the luxury of the furnishings so much as the excellence of the service. The house was crowded. At most of the country inns which we had so far found we were the only guests, and the entire family of the host had usually requisitioned itself into service. Willingness and interest had made up for the few lacks but this home-made machinery might well have broken down if there had been a sudden descent of other guests. At Nirasaki, despite the crowding, we had not to wait an instant for the carrying out of any request. At all times two maids were listening for our handclapping and, for some of the time, three. They added to the customary willingness the knowing how of training. They were, in fact, trained inn *nee-sans*, a class whose manners and morals have been commented upon with some frequency by casual travellers, and it is possible that the outside world's popular judgment of Japanese women has sprung largely from such observations.

In any argument about Japanese morals the likelihood is that the simplest discussion will soon march headlong into a controversy. There arises in a critical comparison of their standards with ours the temptation to assume as a basis our ideal standard against their everyday practice.

The Japanese maid, the daughter of the common people, has been again and again condemned for the easy lightness of her regard for her virtue. I have not found that foreigners who have lived in Japan and who have known the people intimately agree with this sweeping judgment. This charge has grown out of a confusion of possibility with fact. Although we consider that our Western individualism allows far more freedom of choice than does the Eastern family social regulation, particularly in the rigid customs and traditions for women, nevertheless in the morality of sex the guardianship of her chastity by an unmarried Japanese woman of the lower classes is a matter much more of her private concern and nobody else's business than social opinion deems an advisable licence with us. But because the Japanese woman has this freedom it is as absurd to conclude that she makes but one choice as it would be to believe that all order in our society is maintained solely through the police and iron-clad restrictions. When conduct shall be entirely determined by rules, then it will be time to relegate character to the museum.

The duties of the maids of an inn have never included that she must be self-effaced and a silent machine. In the historic friendly relationship between maids and guests there exists a certain standard of manners and good taste, a subtle necessity to the continuance of such existence. One cannot compare the customs of a Japanese inn with the traditions existing in an Occidental hotel. The *nee-san* is unique. When simplicity and naive amusement are spontaneously natural, vulgarity is starved.

After dinner the three maids brought a fresh brewing of tea and teapots filled with iced water. They also brought the message that a travelling theatrical troupe from Tokyo was giving both new and classical plays at the Nirasaki theatre. The actors and actresses were guests under our roof and the mistress of the inn sent the suggestion that the strollers would probably be pleased to entertain us in our room with an act from one of their plays and with dancing and music when they returned at midnight. After our thirty miles in the hot sun the hour of midnight sounded grotesquely post-futuristic. However, it might well have been possible, fortified by tea, iced water, and tobacco, to have awaited the hour if it had not been for another limit to our independence. Temperamentally we might take little heed of the morrow but we had also New England consciences about paying our bills. We could not invite the players to our room without inviting them to a midnight supper, and we knew that the joint treasury could not pay for such a supper.

Thus we made the excuse to the *nee-sans* that their laughter was more pleasing to us than the sound of the *shamisen*. (This statement was not without truth in itself.) The responsibility of amusing us did not seem to weigh heavily upon them. In fact it was we who appeared to be amusing to them. Stupid creatures, we, who could not even play the game of "Stone, Scissors, and Paper!" Our Occidental wits were always a fraction of a second behind. Kenjirō laughed at the bearded Alfred until the toxic of the paroxysm made him delirious. At last we acknowledged the sheerness of our defeats at every venture by sending the victors for ice cream and cakes, and the evening ended with the solemn ceremonial of trying to move the small tin spoons back and forth between plate and lips quickly enough to make a transfer of the frozen mounds before the heat of the tropical night levelled them into liquid.

To escape the midday sun in the short walk to Kōfu, we were off a little after sunrise. Kōfu is more than two thousand feet lower than Fujimi and lies in the heart of a flat valley. It is an ancient city and has not lost its ancient pride, being the wealthy capital of Kai province. We had so much time for the walk that we delayed continually, bargaining in little second-hand shops where the entire stock could hardly have been worth more than a *yen*, and stopping at the coolie tea places where laborers rested to smoke and to mop their faces with pale blue towels. When we were entering Kōfu we were again tempted to halt upon seeing a *kōri* flag floating in the air, proclaiming that an ice supply had arrived. We had not expected to see Kenjirō before we should meet at the inn, but by chance he came wheeling along our street. We called out and he came into our shade. Listeners gathered around our bench, apparently not so much interested in seeing foreigners as in hearing a Japanese speak English.

In the crowd was a very old man, so old that his age seemed pathological rather than human. He made progress by a slow pushing of his feet through the dust. His red-rimmed, staring eyes leered into ours as if we exerted a direct line of magnetism. If we shifted our gaze he immediately shifted around until he again came into vision. Under his arm he carried a long glass bottle, stoppered with a cloth-wound plug. He held up the bottle before us. It was filled with a dirty, pale yellow liquid. Pushed into the bottle was a twisted root holding in the tangle of fibers two or three stones furred with slime. The stones looked somewhat like asbestos.

"What do you think it is?" he asked mysteriously.

We said that we had no idea.

"I wouldn't dare tell you the secret," he went on, "as the bottle is worth five hundred thousand *yen*. If you should pay me a hundred *yen* I would not allow you one taste."

We expressed our happiness that he should have such a fortune. Then he asked if we were Americans and, upon hearing that we were, he formally inquired for an answer as to whether the American nation would buy the bottle. "I can tell you this much," he concluded, "it contains the elixir of eternal life."

The ancient seemed to be such proof in himself that he had lived forever that there was no arguing about eternity with him. For the sake of saying something Kenjirō made the casual guess, "Is it radium?" He was startled into palsy. The crowd stared. Evidently they had heard of radium and it meant magic. Alas! We had gouged out the secret. "Ah-h-h!" he said, "since you know so much, how can you resist the opportunity of living forever?" We explained that under the circumstances of our poverty it looked as if we should have to die along with the rest of the world.

"I have been but testing your faith and knowledge," he said. "The radium of the rocks is permanent. Listen! The bottle may be filled again and again without losing its strength. For only thirty *yen* you may drink."

Forthwith he uncorked the bottle and there escaped an odor so vile that if he had said the tube was the sarcophagus of the lost egg of the great auk we should have believed without dispute. He poured a few drops into a glass and said: "Drink, and you will live forever!"

It is not alone honor that may make one choose death.

The crowd, however, sought eagerly for eternity. They passed the glass around and touched their tongues to the liquid. If any out of the number of that circle escaped typhoid that fact alone ought to convince them of their strength to continue a long way on the road to eternity.

End of the Trail

Whether or no the Bosen-ka inn of Kōfu does possess a wide reputation for comfort, it should deservedly have it. Shio was the name of the maid. This means Salt, but we renamed her "Satō-*san*," which means Miss Sugar. She said that she had been at the inn for fifteen years, but until the day before there had never come a foreigner, and now there were two besides ourselves. I do not understand how such immunity could have been possible in a city the size of Kōfu. However, the fact that there were Occidentals under the roof of the hostelry at that moment was proved by sight and sound. After the many days of hearing only the Japanese cadence, the sound of Western tongues was almost startling. The large room, which became ours, was in the main building and faced the garden. We could look across to the wing where the two foreigners were sitting on their balcony. They were eating tiffin and talking vigorously. One was a short, black-haired, merry Frenchman, the other a tall, blond, closely-cropped German. They spoke either language as the words came. Quite likely they had been in the same university in some European city, and their travelling was a leisurely grand tour. They could not have been hurried or they would not have taken time to search out Kōfu. Their gay spirit was charming. They looked into the eyes of the world with a friendly gaze and the world smiled back at them. Within the month, France and Germany were to declare the implacable war.

High-pitched footbridges linked together the miniature islands of the garden and carried a labyrinthine path over the lotus-covered pond. Lying on the cool, clean mats of our room, sheltered from the sun, the thought of antique shops lured me not. I declared for contemplation, but Kenjirō and Alfred wandered forth. Shio-*san* brought fresh tea and a brazier of glowing charcoal for my pipe. My contemplation began and ended with a luxurious enjoyment of the view of the garden. Through the quiet air came the slow, deep tones of temple gongs. It was a day of special masses. My thoughts found rest in sensuous nothingness and I drifted tranquilly in a glory of inaction. Another day of such devotion to passivity might have started the unfolding within me of the leaves of appreciation for the philosophy of Nirvana, but in the morning some illogical shame for such laziness urged me into joining the pilgrimage of Kenjirō and Alfred to the Shōsenkyō gorge.

The deep, sharp cleft in the granite through which that mountain stream pitches has a rugged beauty. Most perversely, if we had discovered the grandeur for ourselves and had not been over-persuaded by the innkeeper to take the long walk, we would undoubtedly have been more enthusiastic, but as it was we decided that we would rather have spent the day wandering about in Kōfu. Even the unscalable cliffs took on sophistication from the well-worn path below, which proclaimed that the view had been the conventional thing for centuries. Despite all the instruction which the innkeeper had given us about distances and direction, he had escaped correctness in every detail. As often, there was no information obtainable from the heavily-laden coolies tramping along the way. If there is really any mystery which separates East and West it is the East's oblivious indifference to time and space and our complete inability to understand the working of a mind which has over and over again been on a journey and yet has never considered it sufficiently worthwhile to take cognizance either of the distance or the hours.

As we were walking over the flat plain to the beginning of the valley, we stopped for a few minutes to watch a field drill of the conscript army. It was a very hot day, but the uniforms seemed designed for a Manchurian winter. A few of the men had fallen out of the ranks from exhaustion. We heard later that during that hot week in one of the provinces some officer with a new theory had issued an order against the drinking of water during drill, and that the lives of a number of soldiers had been sacrificed to sunstroke. It stirred up an angry scandal. My knowledge of positive thirst would have made me a hanging judge if I had sat on the inquiring court-martial.

We walked on and had forgotten the drill when four or five men and a panting officer overtook us. They entered into a sharp debate with Kenjirō. Finally they dropped behind but followed us until we were a mile away. They had suspected that we were Russian spies.

We lingered in Kōfu for several days but at last again took the old road which runs through the long valleys to Tokyo. This trail from Kōfu on is rather closely followed by the railway just as is the Tōkaidō in the South. I do not know whether it was in honor of (or in disgust at) all such modernities that feudal Edo changed its name to Tokyo. The capital was our destination and we had intended keeping along the direct road but upon a whim (and a look at the map) we suddenly decided to climb the ridge between us and Fuji-*san*, and then to encircle the base of the sacred mountain until we should find again the Tōkaidō which we had forsaken at Nagoya.

It was at the moment of this decision that the demon bicycle collapsed utterly. If it had acquiesced to the change of route it would have had to submit to being carried on the back of a coolie. I have not dared to record all the subtle ingenuities of that mechanical contrivance which it had concocted from time to time to achieve its ends. Its soul had been factoried under a star hostile to human dignity. It could bring about a loss of face to the most innocent who crossed its path. It had the pride of never having been successfully outwitted, and its soul was as proud as the soul of Lucifer. It had no intention of submitting to the indignity of being packed on a coolie nor to have the world see it with its wheels wobbling idly in the air. In desperate determination it committed *harakiri*. Its suicide was heroically completed. As I recorded in the chapter when the bicycle was introduced, Kenjirō gave a shining piece of silver to the coolie to see that the remains had suitable interment. Peace be to those twisted spokes and to that jerry-contraptioned frame!

About noon we found a man with a horse. The man hired himself out to run along behind and Kenjirō mounted the animal. The summit between us and Fuji-*san* was only about three thousand feet above our heads but as we continually had to go down into deep valleys and come up again our ascent took many steps. The thatched villages were very primitive, and the people were very nude. The homes which clung desperately to the edges of the cliffs must have had to breed a special race of children to survive tumbles, just as in the villages below on the shores of the small lakes, they must have had to breed an instinctive knowledge of floating. The houses of those peasants were as much a part of nature as are birds' nests, and they so welded themselves into the unity of the view from the ridges that we did not even think to call them picturesque.

Poor Kenjirō had not a moment when he could sit perpendicularly on his steed. The road was either a scramble or a slide. Finally he dismissed the coolies and the horse. We were at the beginning of a path which was built in sharp zigzags up the side of the mountain. A half-dozen coolie girls with huge chests strapped on their shoulders stopped at a spring and sat down for a moment to fan their flushed, pretty faces. They told us that this was the last climb but they were indefinite about the remaining distance or the time that it would take. It had been our plan to get to the top in time for the sunset view of Fuji-*san* and the lakes. Perhaps the demon bicycle had been granted one last diabolical wish. We were within a few feet of the summit, the air was seemingly clear, when down came a thick, wet cloud from nowhere at all, and our expectation for the crowning glory of the day vanished.

All the way down the other side of the mountain the fog hung over us but it lifted when we reached the shore of Lake Shōji. A village straggled along the water edge. We knew that across the lake was a foreign hotel, but if we had not known it we should nevertheless have had some such suspicion. From the attitude of the villagers it was evident that we had traversed again into tourist territory. The mild, jocular incivility of the natives of any tourist resort any place in the world, except when there is some restraint under the immediacy of employment, is innate and needs no aggravation for its flowering. We were tourists, therefore we must be imbecilic. Derisive hooting followed our ears when we started walking around the lake instead of conventionally taking a boat. Between the fog on the mountain top and our reception in the village we were somewhat out of sympathy with the last hour of the day, and we were even less happy when we reached the hotel, and it was brought to our attention that we had failed to remember that foreign prices prevail at foreign hotels. True, there were excellent reasons why the charges should be higher than at the native inns. The foreign supplies had to be brought long distances on coolie back. This knowledge, however, did not increase the number of *yen* in our pockets. We were in a fitting mood for turning away and pushing on to some isolated village. Such a mood can drive a good bargain and the end was that we were given a room with three iron cots at a minimum charge. I must pay this tribute to that iron cot: I relaxed on its springs in an abandonment to sleep which I shall never forget. But there were other things foreign which were not so pleasant. To have to wait until eight o'clock for a formal dinner when we were accustomed to having meals served at the clapping of our hands, and to have to thump over rough board floors after we had known the refinement of soft matting, and to have to endure all the other half-achieved attempts at foreign service—well, "going native," as the British say in final judgment, "had been the ruining of us."

Waiting until the late foreign breakfast hour in the morning almost numbed the cheerfulness that had risen in me from the exhilarating sleep on the luxurious bed of springs, but the day was shining in such perfection when we found an unfrequented trail north of the chain of lakes, and Fuji-*san* was resting so clearly in the crystal air across the pine tree plain, that we quickly dumped into a maw of forgetfulness any remembrance of such mundane annoyances as foreign hotels. It may have been that volcanic gases were breaking through the clefts in the rocks and that the fumes inspired us with a Delphic madness. Our mood became ecstatic. We unburdened ourselves of wild and soaring theories of art and religion, of love and life— and there were theories that came forth which we had never dreamed existed in cosmos. We scattered these inspired words in wanton waste as if we were on a journey to some world where such wealth would be dross.

The town which we found for the night was on what is called "the Shōji-route around Fuji-*san*." We avoided the semi-foreign hotel but that did not save us from being tourists. The native inn had ready for us in the morning a bill almost twice as large as it should have been. In consequence we added no "tea-money." If we had, we should have gone from the village penniless. In all our wandering this was the first deliberate overcharge, and in one way it may have been justified in the opinion of the mistress. She had probably learned from the semi-foreign hotel across the street that foreigners know not the custom of tea-money and ignorantly pay only the bill that is presented without adding a suitable and proportionate present.

Truly we were now in the domain not only of the foreign tourist but of the native pilgrim as well. All day we walked through the towns which serve as starting points for the different routes of ascent for Fuji-san. It was the height of the season for the sacred climb and the towns, purveying every imaginable necessity and souvenir, had mushroomed into crowded camps. We were unworthy guests. As far as our purchasing ability was concerned, a postcard was an outside luxury. When we reached Gotenba we sat down for a conference, following the rule of "when in doubt drink a pot of tea."

By rail to Yokohama was fifty-one miles. We had leisurely covered about twenty-five miles that day. Even if we should make ten or fifteen miles more before night, there would be a sufficiently long, scorching, penniless day to come. The country was not new to us as we had both tramped through the exploited Miyanoshita and Kamakura districts. "Since these things are so," I argued, "let's use our remaining coppers to buy tickets on the express to Yokohama." As no one's pride sufficiently demanded that we had to take the fifty-one miles on foot, this plan was our final agreement.

Our linen suits were perhaps not as freshly laundered as those of the other haughty *seiyō-jin* who were riding on the first and second-class cars of the train, but otherwise our poverty did not particularly proclaim itself. We walked to our hotel in Yokohama and took rooms, relying that future funds would come out of the letter which was supposedly waiting at the bank for me. In the meantime in the bag which had been forwarded from Nagoya I found a two-dollar American bill. This gift we cashed into *yen* and sat through the evening on a terrace over the bund along the water front, sipping forgotten coffee and ordering long, iced, fresh lemon drinks. A steamer had landed that day and at the next table to ours was a charming group of American girls. They were filled with enthusiasm for the exotic. The soft, evening air, the passing life along the street, and the gay tables carried me back to my own first night in Japan, which had been spent eleven years before on that very terrace.

The hoped-for letter was waiting for me at the bank. The amount above the exact sum necessary for my steamship ticket had been intended for insurance against extras. It was now necessary for mere existence. We entered into an infinite calculation of finance down to the ultimate *sen*. Yokohama was no place for economy and we shook off its dust for that of Tokyo and were happy again in a native inn. With our linen suits laundered, we called on old friends and shopped betimes on credit. It was a rather queer sensation to be bargaining for luxuries when a mere *bona fide* payment of a *rikisha* charge meant a most delicate readjustment of our entire capital. Dealers were quite willing to forward boxes to America with hardly more guarantee than our promise to pay sometime. I felt that if we were to ask them suddenly for ten *yen* in cash our credit would have crashed to earth. Nevertheless we were confident of our dole outlasting our needs. We lived our moments gaily. We saved *yen* to pay the inn bill, and our boat was scheduled to sail on a certain day.

Kenjirō was determined that our last day should be worthy and memorable. Through friends he arranged that we should meet Count Ōkuma Shigenobu, the Premier of the Empire. We had made most of our visits about the city on foot, and on one of the hottest days we had walked the round trip of a dozen miles to have afternoon tea with a former Japanese diplomat to America and his family, trusting that his sense of humor would forgive our perspiration, but one does not arrive thus at a palace door. Great was the excitement at the inn when *rikisha* men were called and our destination was given out. We dashed away and careened around the corners at tremendous speed. It was at least the second hottest day of the year, but the coolies realized that they were part of a ceremony and that their duty was to arrive streaming, panting, and exhausted.

Count Ōkuma, on his son's arm, entered the small reception room into which we were shown. (The bullet of a fanatic shattered the bone of his leg when he was a young man.) Count Ōkuma is almost the last survivor of that group who directed the miracle of transforming the Japan of feudalism into the modern nation.

We drank tea and asked formal questions. Following some turn of the conversation—Count Ōkuma was speaking of loyalty—we inquired, as we had of the ancient schoolmaster of Kami-Suwa: "Can virtue be taught?"

The expression in the eyes of the Premier's great, handsome head had been passive as he had acquiesced in what had been said up to that time. Now his expression became positive. He spoke slowly as if he were summing up the belief and experience of a lifetime.

"When Japan, after her centuries of hermitage, had suddenly either to face the West and to compete successfully with you, or to sink into being a tributary and exploited people, our greatest necessity in patriotism was to recognize instantly that in the physical and material world we had to learn everything from you. Our social, commercial, and governmental methods were suited only to the organization of society which we then had. We discovered that your world is a world of commerce and competition, that the achieving of wealth from the profits of trade demands training, efficiency, ingenuity, and initiative. Our civilization had not developed these qualities in us. We could only hope that we had latent ability. Furthermore, observation of you taught us to realize the value of physical power. We saw that mere superior cleverness and ability in the competition to live is not sufficient until backed by a preparedness of force. America was our great teacher and we shall never cease to be grateful. In the physical world we had everything to learn from you, and today we must constantly remember that we have only begun to learn.

"It was our overwhelming task to begin at the beginning, and we should have had no success if it had not been for the moral qualities of the Japanese people. These virtues cannot be taught—merely as they are required. They are the spiritual and moral inheritage from the past. In the avalanche of Western ideas which came upon us, it was our great work to pick, to choose, and to adapt. These ideas were the ideas of the commercial world. There are those who say that Japan in taking over these standards of materialism relinquished the priceless inheritance of its own spiritual life. No! We have had *everything* to learn from you in methods, but that should not be confused with spiritual values. I do not mean mere creeds and dogma, but to the essence, the great fundamentals of all true religion.

"It is possible that sometime in the future the outside world may discover that it will have need to come to us for the values that are ours through our great moral inheritance of loyalty. In a material way we can never pay back to you our obligation for having been taught your material lessons. But it may be that Western nations have put too great faith in materialism and that they will arrive at the bitter knowledge that the fruit of life is death unless the faith of men reaches out for something beyond the material. Then, if we of Japan have humbly guarded our spiritual wealth, the world may come to ask the secret of our spiritual values as we went to you to ask the inner secret of your material values."

Beach Combers

On the morning the boat was to sail from Yokohama we were up as soon as the sun first came through the bamboo shades. We exchanged presents with everyone in the inn and then walked away to the station, and everyone from the aristocratic mistress to the messenger boy stood waving to us as long as we could turn back to see them. Our packages and presents half filled the car. Kenjirō had had a telegram to hurry home. The train was a through express to Kyoto and we said "*sayōnara*" to him from the Yokohama platform.

We went to the bank and I exchanged my receipt for the envelope which held the money for my steamer ticket. In our treasury was left one last Japanese note which we had been saving as a margin. We now thought it was safely ours to spend as we might choose. We went to find some very particular incense and some very particular tea which a Japanese acquaintance had discovered and had given us the address of. We plunged almost to the limit of the note.

"Haven't you heard that your boat has been held up forty-eight hours in Kobe?" asked the steamship agent.

We had heard no such news, but we were interested. To be able to have, when one might wish to make the choice, the gift of forty-eight hours in Japan would be one sort of a blessing. At that particular moment the prospect had complications. Until that instant our system of finance had been the pride of our hearts. We had calculated so admirably that we had retained just one *yen* for porters' fees at the dock.

Alfred had his return ticket. "Can't I pay for my ticket in part by cheque?" I asked.

After consultation in the inner office the agent returned and announced, "No, that isn't done."

The agent and his advisers thought that if I should happen to fall overboard there might be a legal complication with my estate——if I happened to have an estate.

"Your records show," I argued, "that my friend has crossed on your line three times. Discounting any other substantiality, at least that proves that one of us has had practice in not tumbling overside."

Evidently my logic was at fault. From the dubious looks that came across the desk I judged that the agent was thinking that such fly-like pertinacity of sticking aboard a vessel was suspicious and unnatural in a passenger.

"Well," said Alfred as we walked away, "you've wondered what it would be like to be an amateur beach comber. Now is your admirable chance."

Alfred seemed to forget that he was in no better position than was I in regard to funds.

The day before we had had tea with the Premier of Japan. Now we faced forty-eight hours of starvation. Our horoscopes evidently had been cast that we were to be beach combers, the admirable chance of which Alfred had suggested.

We did not deceive ourselves that our few hours of homelessness made us professionals, nevertheless we were given a picture impression of Yokohama that could only have been bought by hunger and sleeplessness. We saw the going to bed of the city, and we saw its getting up. We saw Theatre Street gay with lanterns and filled with merrymakers. Hours later we saw the lanterns go out and the waiters and waitresses come forth to crowd into the public baths. We walked through the glitter of the street which winds between the houses of the wall-imprisoned Yoshiwara district. There is but one entrance to this district——a long stone bridge. We saw that bridge again, at the hour of sunrise. It was then crowded with beggars and loathsome hangers-on, waiting to importune the exodus. Vice by grey daylight is horrible, and those brilliant palaces of the night before bulked in a row of dull and sinister ugliness in the half daylight. Back and forth we explored the streets of the city. We passed a foreign sailors' low dive, and a toothless old woman and a leering youth grabbed at our arms and invited us in. They spoke phrases of English. There was wild laughter and music on the upper floor.

Sometimes the hours went quickly, sometimes they lingered interminably with no seeming relation between their speeding and the interest of the moment. Sometimes we were hungry and sometimes we forgot our hunger. We found a small park near the foreign settlement with benches admirable for sleeping if it had not been for the diligence of the sand fleas and the gnats. From the park we walked down along the bund and on the promenade facing the harbour we found two seats. A Japanese sailor was sitting on one.

We wished him good-evening and shared with him our cigarettes. After a time we wandered away to walk again through the streets of the bright lanterns. We had been refusing *rikisha* men for so many hours that the guild at last seemed to remember us as non-possibilities, that is, all except one man who persisted in turning up at every corner. He spoke some English and had a new suggestion for his every proposal. If ever a coolie looked theatrically villainous, it was that coolie. Furthermore, he was half-drunk from cheap *sake*. Eventually he discovered a companion and the two of them settled down at our heels. Whenever we hesitated they threw their *rikisha* shafts across our path. They thought that we were officers from some ship and they were counting upon our having to return before the four-o'clock watch. I do not know that officers ever do have to return at that hour, but the coolies were sure that we had such necessity. When four o'clock came they were mystified and angry. Until then they had rather amused us. We now told them to be off and we walked away into the quiet streets. They still persisted in their following. We tried indifference and we tried invective. I could see that the police at the corners were watching the procession. We might have appealed to them, but one seldom appeals to the police in a foreign land, especially in Japan, if there is any question of time to be considered. We had to take the boat the next morning. We had no desire to be ordered to report the next day at a police station. And for that matter, I should hardly have felt like criticizing any officer for deciding to lock us all up together. The coolies might have appealed that we had hired them and had not paid them. Anyhow, why should two foreigners be wandering around in questionable districts at such an hour of the night? If there had to be a settlement with our pair of villains, it was just as well to have it beyond the eye of the law.

Our next move was melodramatic. We drew a line across the road and when our parasites caught up we told them that they crossed that line at their peril. Just what we should have done if they had crossed the line I have no idea. We walked along pleased with the result of our ultimatum until, ten or fifteen minutes later, I happened to turn around and again saw the two men, this time without their *rikisha*.

We were now headed toward the sea front by way of the foreign sections. The buildings were absolutely dark but there was an occasional street light. If there were any watchmen they were within the walls. We had walked through the narrow streets of that district so often that we remembered the turns. We felt sure that the men could not catch up with us except from behind. We were well out on the bund before they came out of the alley that we had left. They were both carrying sticks, which looked like *rikisha* shafts, and the second man had a knife.

We walked along toward the benches where we had been sitting earlier in the night. Steamer lights were twinkling on the harbour and Alfred pointed out our ship waiting to dock at sunrise. Years before I had been attacked in the streets of San Francisco, but that assault had been so sudden that there was no anticipatory excitement. Our Yokohama anticipatory reflection was the amusing idea that if the knaves should attain the triumph of searching our pockets they would have a most disheartening anti-climax after all their evening's trouble.

Just as we reached the benches they came for us. We stepped around the first bench to break the charge. Outstretched on the bench was our Japanese sailor whom we had helped out with cigarettes. He may have been asleep, but when he jumped to his feet he was very wide awake. Without waiting for particulars he whipped out a clasp knife. We had been friends and this was a chance to even up his obligation to us. The two coolies stopped as if they had run against an invisible wire. We stood facing each other, and then, as stealthily as a great cat, the sailor began moving forward. He walked very slowly but he seemed to thirst to use his knife. Even with three to two, I felt that the coolies, half-drunken, would have tried to hold their ground if it had not been for the sailor's uncanny deliberation. They waited for him to come no nearer. They fled. We could hear them running long after the darkness closed them in.

We tried to express our appreciation to the sailor for his interest. He made some answer which sounded as if he were bored.

One place and another we had found a little sleep in the two days but the thought of a soft, clean steamer bunk began to form itself in my brain and the first sign of the sun was truly welcome. We turned back to the city for one last long walk over the heights. The town was sleepily waking up. The streets that had been the darkest in the night were now the busiest. Our walk ended at the parcel room of the railway station where we had left our rucksacks. The boy who was sweeping out the station restaurant allowed us to shave and scrub behind a screen and make ourselves somewhat presentable for the boat.

Our luggage, which had been in storage, was on the dock waiting for us. Alfred thoroughly shook the linen envelope which had so long been our treasury but the yield refused to increase beyond three silver ten-*sen* pieces. I once saw an Italian in Venice fee an entire hotel line with a few coppers. He accomplished the act with such graceful courtesy that seemingly the servants were appreciative of the spirit of the giving rather than the value of the coins. I tried to distribute our pieces of silver to the porters on the dock with an air copied from my remembrance of the Italian, and the Japanese recipients entered into the drama with sufficient make-belief to have saved our faces if it had not been for the chill in the critical eyes of two English sailors standing at the gangplank. The implication of their Anglo-Saxon hauteur was that it might be satisfying to the heathen in their darkness to weigh in with the heft of compensation such useless freight as palaver and smiles, but as for them, they belonged to a civilization preferring less manners and more substance.

As the boat swung from the pier and open water began to show, a man came running down the dock waving the copy of a cablegram. "Germany has invaded France and England may declare war," he shouted. Yes, decidedly our days of turning back the clock were over. We were no longer *rōnin* wandering in feudal Japan. We had left the Two-Sworded Trails and were back in the civilization of the two English sailors.

Slowly the harbour of Yokohama was curtained and disappeared behind a brightly glistening mist. I stood against the rail trying to think of America and Europe. My mind had that illusory, abnormal clearness which sometimes follows days without sleep. I stood, thinking, thinking, the first beginning of that agony of trying to add a cubit to our vision by thought.

Glossary

akanbō:	Baby.
banzai:	Hurray.
bentō:	A lunch.
bushidō:	The Way of the warrior.
daimyō:	Feudal lord.
furo:	Bath.
furoshiki:	Wrapping cloth.
fusuma:	Sliding door covered with thick paper.
geisha:	A woman professionally trained to entertain customers with music, dancing, food and drinks, and witty stories.
geta:	Wooden clogs.
harakiri:	Ritual suicide.
hibachi:	Brazier.
jūjūtsu:	The art of self-decence without weapons.
kakemono:	Hanging scroll.
kebukai:	Hairy.
kimono:	Traditional female garment.
kirei:	Beautiful.
kisha:	(Steam) train.
kōri:	Ice.
musume:	Daughter (girl).
nee-san:	Older sister (young girl working at an inn).
netsuke:	Small figure of ivory, wood, metal, or ceramic, used as a buttonlike fixture on a man's sash.

nomi-yoke:	Flee-repellant.
obi:	Belt.
o-hayō:	Good morning.
o-yasumi nasai:	Goo night.
o-yu:	Hot water.
ramune:	Carbonated soft drink.
ri:	2.44 miles.
rikisha:	Rickshaw.
rōnin:	Masterless samurai.
sake:	Japanese rice wine.
samurai:	Warrior.
sayōnara:	Goodbye.
seiyō-jin:	Westerner.
shamisen:	Three-stringed musical instrument.
shōgun:	Hereditary military ruler during Japan's feudal era.
shōji:	Lightweight sliding doors covered with paper.
tabi:	Traditional socks with separated pouch for the big toe.
yadoya:	Japanese-style inn.
yukata:	Informal light cotton *kimono*.

Index

TOYO Press publishes books that contribute to a deeper understanding of Asian cultures. Editorial supervision: William de Lange. Book and cover design: Chōkei Studios. Printing and binding: IngramSpark. The typefaces used are Perpetua, Prescript, and Herculanum.